Airliners of the 2000s

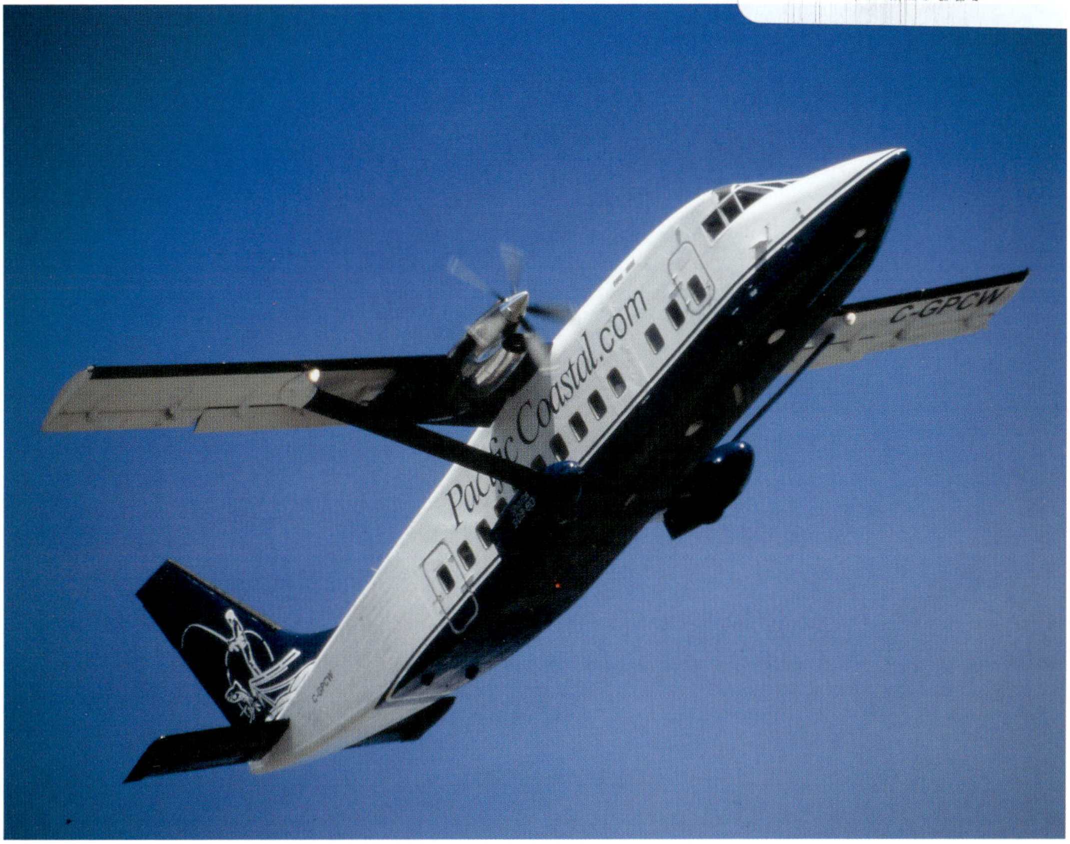

GERRY MANNING

Key Books

HISTORIC COMMERCIAL AIRCRAFT SERIES, VOLUME 5

Acknowledgements

Thanks to Bob O'Brien for his extra work on the scanned slides and for proofreading the text.

Tails of Hong Kong – a mix of operators from mainland China, Japan, Dubai and Hong Kong are parked at their gates.

Published by Key Books
An imprint of Key Publishing Ltd
PO Box 100
Stamford
Lincs PE19 1XQ

www.keypublishing.com

The right of Gerry Manning to be identified as the author of this book has been asserted in accordance with the Copyright, Designs and Patents Act 1988 Sections 77 and 78.

Copyright © Gerry Manning, 2022

ISBN 978 1 80282 256 4

All rights reserved. Reproduction in whole or in part in any form whatsoever or by any means is strictly prohibited without the prior permission of the Publisher.

Typeset by SJmagic DESIGN SERVICES, India.

Introduction

This is the fifth book in my series, Airliners of the Decade. The first, *Airliners of the 1960s*, was published by Airlife in 2000; the second and third, *Airliners of the 1970s* and *Airliners of the 1980s*, were published by Midland Publishing in 2005 and 2007, respectively; and the fourth, *Airliners of the 1990s*, was pubished by Key Publishing in 2021. This latest work follows the same premise, to illustrate the range of both airliners and airlines that operated during the decade. It is, of course, impossible within the scope of a book of this size to cover all the carriers and types of aircraft to be seen during those years. However, I have aimed to cover a wide selection of aircraft and airlines across a large geographical spread – from the small commuter aeroplanes to the large multi-engine, wide-bodied aircraft.

As through all decades, there were many important developments during the 2000s. One such development was the Airbus consortium becoming the major producer of airliners in the world and out-selling Boeing, and, on a negative note, it was the decade that saw the end of supersonic travel for the public, with Concorde being taken out of service. For the enthusiast, it was perhaps the last decade that the airliners from the former Union of Soviet Socialist Republics (USSR) were still to be found in some numbers, with most in the livery of the many new airlines and nations that grew out of its demise. I could not resist adding as many as possible.

In the captions, I have attempted to say what the airline was (or still is), the type of aircraft, and where and when the picture was taken. Lastly, I outline the fate of the illustrated aircraft. Since most aircraft are now leased rather than bought by airlines, there is a tendency to break up some airframes much earlier than would have happened in the past. This is because, in some cases, the aircraft is worth more for the sum of all its spare parts than as a complete unit. When an aircraft was moved to another airline, I have used the words 'sold on'; this covers both actual sales and it moving to a new lease.

The COVID-19 pandemic has left its mark on commercial aviation, and now, albeit slowly, services are beginning to climb back the levels of 2019, before the virus struck. Many types, however, especially the less fuel efficient, have gone into store and may never return to service.

All the pictures are from my own travels and scanned from Fujichrome slides.

Gerry Manning, Liverpool
March 2022

Airliners of the 2000s

In its heyday, during the 1960s, the Boeing 707 was the most popular long-haul airliner of that era. By the start of the new millennium, the 707 was getting quite rare, and those that were to be found still in operation were converted to haul cargo and not passengers. Pictured in March 2000, climbing out of Sharjah International Airport, United Arab Emirates (UAE), is Boeing 707-366C SU-APD c/n 20341 of Cairo-based Egypt Air, that nation's flag carrier. This aircraft was sold in 2004 to another Egyptian carrier and later broken up.

The most produced version of the 707 was the -300 long-range intercontinental variant. It was this model that most of the 707s seen in the first decade of the 2000s came from. Boeing 707-330C ST-AKW c/n 20123 of Azza Air Transport, based at Khartoum, Sudan, is seen on the runway at Sharjah International Airport in March 2000. In October 2009, the aircraft crashed just after take-off at this location, and the carrier ceased operations in 2013.

Boeing 707-321C HS-TFS c/n 19372 of Bangkok-based Thai Flying Services is pictured on the ramp at Sharjah International Airport in March 2000. This was the only large airframe in the company fleet, which today consists of only small aircraft. This 707 was sold on to an operator in Guinea-Bissau and registered in the Cook Islands. In October 2009, it was written off at Mombasa, Kenya; when landing, it hit the landing lights, and the right-hand undercarriage collapsed, causing damage beyond economic repair.

The original Boeing 717 was the initial designation for the KC-135A aerial in-flight refuelling tanker for the US Air Force. However, since this type did not enter commercial service, it was not used in practice. Following the 1997 takeover of McDonnell Douglas by Boeing, the company decided to rebrand the MD-95-30 with a Boeing number, so it reused the 717 title. Pictured on approached to Palma de Mallorca Airport, Spain, in September 2000, is Boeing 717-2CM EC-HOA c/n 55061 of AeBal (Aerolineas Baleares). The Palma-based airline ceased operations in September 2008, and this aircraft was sold on to an operator in Sweden, then one in Finland, and is now in store.

Based in the city of its name, Bangkok Air today brands itself as a 'boutique airline', and, since it operates to Thailand's holiday resorts, it paints its aircraft in bright colours. Seen at Don Muang International Airport, Bangkok, in January 2002, is Boeing 717-23S HS-PGP c/n 55064. This aircraft was sold on to an operator in Spain and then one in Finland; in October 2020, it was withdrawn from use in Blytheville, Arkansas.

For many years, TWA (Trans World Airlines) was one of two, alongside Pan American, American airlines that operated worldwide. In 2001, it was taken over and absorbed into American Airlines. Seen at Minneapolis-St Paul International Airport, in May 2000, is Boeing 717-231 N402TW c/n 55069 of TWA. This aircraft was sold on to another American carrier and put into store in San Bernardino, California, in 2021.

Pictured at Detroit Metropolitan Airport, in August 2008, is Boeing 717-2BD N922AT c/n 55050 of Atlanta-based AirTran Airways. The carrier was taken over by Southwest Airlines in May 2011, and this aircraft was sold on and later put into store in San Bernardino, California, in January 2021.

The Boeing 727 was a mid-range, jet-powered airliner with the ability to operate from smaller airports with less ground-support equipment. It first flew in 1963 and featured three Pratt & Whitney JT8D-7 turbofans, two mounted on the rear fuselage and the third below the fin. Seen on the move at Lima Jorge Chávez International Airport, in October 2003, is Boeing 727-22 OB-1546-P c/n 19150 of Aero Continente. The Peruvian carrier lost its certificate to operate the following year. Later, it was bought out by the staff and resumed services. In 2005, the certificate was once again revoked. This aircraft was withdrawn from use at the airline's Lima base in 2004 and stored.

By the start of the 2000s, many 727s had been converted to freighters. Pictured at Edmonton International Airport, Alberta, in September 2008, is Boeing 727-22C C-GHWC c/n 19195 of Westcan International Airlines. The Edmonton-based carrier ceased operations in 2010, and this aircraft was sold to an operator in the Democratic Republic of the Congo and is currently preserved in a park in the capital, Kinshasa.

Many popular airliners were deemed to be too small for their operators, and so it was for the original -100 727. The answer from the manufacturer was to add two 10ft (3.05m) fuselage sections, one in front and the other aft of the wing. These enlarged aircraft became the -200 series. Seen arriving at Harry Mwanga Nkumbula International Airport, Livingstone, Zambia, in September 2006, is Boeing 727-281 ZS-OZP c/n 20572 of Johannesburg-based Nationwide Airlines. This aircraft was configured for passengers with 12 business class seats and 135 economy seats. It was withdrawn from use later that year and broken up.

Seen at Dubai International Airport, in November 2008, is Boeing 727-228 EP-ASC c/n 22084 of Iran Aseman Airlines. The Tehran-based carrier still operates this aircraft.

Pictured on the ramp at Sharjah International Airport, in March 2000, is Boeing 727-243F VT-LCC c/n 22167, operated by Hinduja Cargo Services. The carrier was owned by Delhi-based Lufthansa Cargo India. Operations were suspended in August of that year. This aircraft was sold on to a company in Brazil and by 2015 had been broken up.

Airliners of the 2000s

Heading a line of four, in September 2005, is Boeing 727-223(F) C-FCJP c/n 22012 of Cargojet Airways at the company base of John C. Munro Hamilton International Airport, Ontario. The carrier is still current today, but this aircraft was put into store in April 2009 and broken up.

For many years, the Boeing 737 was the world's best-selling jet airliner in terms of numbers. The original -100 series only had a production run of 30, as most airline customers needed a bigger aircraft. The -200 was longer by 78in (1.93m) and could seat up to 130 passengers. The -200 first entered service in April 1968. Pictured on approach to Manchester Airport, in March 2002, is Boeing 737-204 EI-CJD c/n 22966 of Dublin-based Ryanair. Today, the carrier is one of the largest in Europe. This aircraft is painted as a flying billboard to advertise the Irish mobile telephone company Eircell. It was withdrawn from service in 2004 and used for fire practice at Dublin Airport.

Pictured at Santiago de Chile Airport, in October 2003, is Boeing 737-2H6 CC-CTO c/n 20583 of Sky Airlines. The carrier is based at Santiago, and this aircraft was sold on to a carrier in Peru and eventually withdrawn from use.

On the ramp at Punta del Este International Airport, named after the holiday resort town it serves, in October 2003, is Boeing 737-2A3 CX-BON c/n 22737, operated by the national flag carrier PLUNA Lineas Aéreas Uruguayas. Government-owned, the Montevideo-based carrier was closed down in July 2012. This aircraft was put into store in October 2008, and ten years later it was preserved in Costa Rica as a restaurant.

Boeing 737-228 LV-ZXB c/n 23009 of Austral Líneas Aéreas is at the company base at Buenos Aires Aeroparque Jorge Newbery in October 2003. The carrier was a subsidiary of Aerolíneas Argentina and was merged into the main company in 2020. This aircraft was put into store late in 2009.

Seen climbing out of Vancouver International Airport, in August 2005, is Boeing 737-269 C-GWJK c/n 21206 of Calgary-based WestJet Airlines, one of Canada's leading low-cost carriers. This early 737 was withdrawn from use at Walnut Ridge, Arkansas.

On the ramp at Yellowknife Airport, Northwest Territories (NWT), in September 2008, is Boeing 737-217 C-GKCP c/n 22729 of Canadian North. The company operates from its Yellowknife base and flies to many locations in the far north of Canada. This aircraft has been withdrawn from use.

On the move to take off, in October 2003, at Lima Jorge Chávez International Airport, is Boeing 737-244 OB-1713 c/n 19707, operated by TANS (Transportes Aéreos Nacionales de la Selva), a division of the Peruvian Air Force. Based at Lima, the division's role was to operate services around the vast nation that would not be economical to a commercial carrier. Operations ceased in January 2006, and this aircraft joined the Peruvian Air Force and was later written off.

First flown in February 1984, the 737-300 series was Boeing's logical progression of improvement of the best-selling -200 series. It was longer by 44in (1.11m) forward and 60in (1.52m) aft of the wing, as well as having extended wingtips. The biggest change was a completely new powerplants, a CFM-56 with a thrust of 22,100lb st. The aircraft no longer featured a round nacelle holding the engine but had a more oval shaped one, as otherwise there would not have been sufficient ground clearance. Seen at Brisbane Airport, in February 2003, is Boeing 737-3K2 ZK-SJE c/n 27635 of Freedom Air International, which is based in Auckland, New Zealand. The carrier ceased operations in March 2008, and this aircraft can now be found operating in Kyrgyzstan.

Pictured on the move at Tel Aviv Ben Gurion International Airport, in June 2008, is Boeing 737-3Y0 EI-DJS c/n 23926 of KD Avia (Kaliningrad Avia). The aircraft is leased, hence the Irish registration. The Kaliningrad-based carrier suspended operations in September of the following year, and this aircraft was withdrawn from service.

Seen arriving at Melbourne Tullamarine Airport, in February 2003, is Boeing 737-36Q ZK-NGB c/n 29140 of Air New Zealand, the Auckland-based flag carrier. This aircraft was sold on and now operates in Canada.

Pictured at Dubai International Airport, in November 2008, is Boeing 737-340 AP-BCA c/n 23294 of Karachi-based Pakistan International Airlines, the nation's flag carrier. In 2013, this aircraft was withdrawn from service.

For the -400 series 737, Boeing once again extended the fuselage, this time by 66in (1.67m) forward and 48in (1.21m) aft of the wing. It first flew in February 1988 and could carry up to 168 passengers, depending upon the airline's configuration. Boeing 737-4Q8 SX-BKH c/n 24703 of Athens-based Olympic Airlines is at Berlin Tegel Airport, in May 2008. This airport has now closed. The following year, the Greek government sold its interest in the carrier to a private investment company, and operations ceased at the end of September. The carrier, now operating under the name Olympic Air, resumed flying in October. This aircraft was put into store at Roswell, New Mexico, in 2010 and later broken up.

Seen at a wet Naha Airport, Okinawa, Japan, in October 2004, is Boeing 737-446 JA8994 c/n 28097 of JAL Express. The carrier was owned by Japan Airlines (JAL) and was merged into the main company in September 2014. This aircraft now operates for a Greek company.

Being pushed back from its gate at Naha Airport, Okinawa, in October 2004, is Boeing 737-4K5 JA8934 c/n 27830 of JTA (Japan Transocean Air). The company is owned by JAL and based in Okinawa. This aircraft was sold on and now operates in China.

Heading a line of three, in February 2003, is Boeing 737-4U3 PK-GWQ c/n 25719 of Garuda Indonesia Airways. It is not at the company's current Jakarta base but at Singapore Changi Airport. This aircraft has since joined the Indonesian Air Force.

Arriving at its gate, in February 2003, at Sydney Kingsford Smith Airport, is Boeing 737-4L7 VH-RON c/n 26960 of Air Nauru. Nauru is a tiny island nation in Micronesia, northeast of Australia. This aircraft was sold on to South Africa, and, in October 2015, it was damaged beyond economic repair when landing at Johannesburg, following the collapse of the left-hand undercarriage.

On the move at Tokyo Haneda Airport, in October 2004, is Boeing 737-4YO JA737E c/n 26069 of SNA (Skynet Asia Airways). Based in Miyazaki, the company was rebranded as Solaseed Air in July 2011. Sold on, this aircraft currently operates in Spain.

The -500 variant of the 737 did not follow the 'bigger is better' policy, instead reverting back down to the size of the -200, with just an extension of 19in (47cm). The reason for this is that not all airlines wanted the larger machines, but they did want the new engines. Pictured at Zürich Airport, in September 2004, is Boeing 737-530 OK-SWY c/n 24815 of Smart Wings, the low-cost scheduled service division of Prague-based Travel Service. In 2015, this aircraft was preserved by Lufthansa at its Hamburg training centre and used to teach engineers their trade.

Seen at a snowy Salzburg W. A. Mozart Airport, in January 2006, is Boeing 737-5YO OM-SEA c/n 25186 of Bratislava-based SkyEurope Airlines. Slovakia had only been formed in 1993, when it peacefully split from the Czech Republic. The airline suspended operations in September 2009, and this aircraft was sold on; after service in Russia, it went into store in Ardmore, Oklahoma, in 2019.

Airliners of the 2000s

On pushback from its gate at Manchester Airport's Terminal 1, in April 2001, is Boeing 737-55S OK-XGE c/n 26543 of CSA (Czech Airlines), the Prague-based national flag carrier. This aircraft became a technical training airframe, in Nanjing, for China Southern Airlines in 2020.

Pictured on the move at Singapore Changi Airport, in February 2003, is Boeing 737-524 XU-735 c/n 26319 of Mekong Airlines, based in Phnom Penh, Cambodia. Three months later, the company suspended operations. Sold on, this aircraft was in store in Minsk, Belarus, by 2021.

Boeing 737-53A VP-BFM c/n 24921 of Russian holiday airline Sky Express is pictured at the company's base of Moscow Vnukovo International Airport, in August 2007. In October 2011, the company ceased operations, and this aircraft was broken up at Durham Tees Valley Airport, UK.

Seen from the balcony at Warsaw Chopin Airport, in June 2008, is Boeing 737-53S YL-BBE c/n 29073 of Air Baltic, Latvia's flag carrier, which is based in Riga. Sold on, this aircraft now operates in Nigeria.

The -600 variant of the 737 was one of the 'Next Generation' series of the type. It was designed to replace the -500 version and featured a new 'glass cockpit' for the pilots, with electronic flight instruments. The wingspan was increased by 16ft 5in (5.04m), and the prototype first flew in January 1998. Pictured at Warsaw Chopin Airport, in June 2008, is Boeing 737-683 LN-RPU c/n 28312 of SAS (Scandinavian Airlines System), the flag carrier for Sweden, Norway and Denmark. This aircraft was broken up in St Athan, UK, in 2014. Boeing no longer offers the -600 to customers.

First flown in February 1997, the -700 variant of the 737 was the 'Next Generation' airframe designed to replace the -300, having the same improvements as the -600. Pictured arriving at Melbourne Tullamarine Airport, in February 2003, is Boeing 737-7X2 DQ-FJF c/n 28878 of Air Pacific, which is based in Suva, Fiji. The carrier was rebranded in June 2013 as Fiji Airlines, and this aircraft was broken up in 2020 at Durham Tees Valley Airport.

On the move at Brisbane Airport, in February 2003, is Boeing 737-7BX VH-VBP c/n 30743 of Virgin Blue Airlines. Locally based, the company was rebranded as Virgin Australia in 2011. This aircraft was sold on in Europe and later broken up.

Lining up to take off on Manchester Airport's runway 23L, in August 2003, is Boeing 737-75B D-AGES c/n 28108 of Hapag-Lloyd Express, based in Langenhagen, Germany. This was a no-frills, high-frequency airline, which became part of TUIfly along with its parent company, Hapag-Lloyd Flug, in January 2007. This aircraft was broken up in 2019.

Boeing 737-7H4 N755SA c/n 27871 of Dallas Love Field-based Southwest Airlines approaches to land, in October 2001, at Los Angeles International Airport (LAX). The carrier is the one that wrote the 'textbook' of how to run a low-cost, no-frills airline, which almost all others try to copy. This aircraft still serves with this carrier.

The -800 series of the 737 was the 'Next Generation' variant designed to replace the -400. Seen at Warsaw Chopin Airport, in June 2008, is Boeing 737-86N SU-BPZ c/n 35213 of Cairo-based AMC Aviation (Aircraft Maintenance Company). The aircraft still serves with them.

Seen arriving at Dubai International Airport, in November 2008, is Boeing 737-81M A40-BR c/n 33104 of Muscat-based Oman Air, the nation's flag carrier. This aircraft was sold on and now operates in Spain.

On the move at Hong Kong Chek Lap Kok Airport in March 2003, is Boeing 737-81B B-2694 c/n 32922 of Guangzhou-based China Southern Airlines. This aircraft still serves with the carrier.

In a special livery to advertise the mobile telephone network of Telefonica/O$_2$ is Boeing 737-86Q OK-TVC c/n 30278 of Prague-based Travel Service. It is pictured at Brno-Tuřany Airport, Czech Republic, in September 2008. The carrier was renamed Smart Wings, the name of its low-cost subsidiary, in December 2018. This aircraft was sold on and now operates in the UK.

Air India Express is a Mumbai-based low-cost division of parent company Air India. All the aircraft have different tail artwork. Seen at Dubai International Airport, in November 2008, is Boeing 737-8HG VT-AXP c/n 36328. This aircraft still serves with the company.

First flown in August 2000, the -900 variant of the 737 was the longest of them all at 138ft 2in (42.1m). It is interesting to note that the original -100 version was just 94ft (28.65m) long. Seen about to be pushed back from its gate at Amsterdam Schiphol Airport, in June 2007, is Boeing 737-9K2 PH-BXS c/n 29602 of Dutch flag carrier KLM (Koninklijke Luchtvaart Maatschappij, Royal Dutch Airlines). This aircraft still serves with the company.

Best known as the 'jumbo jet', the Boeing 747 went on to change the face of travel for both the airlines and the travelling public, as it made long-haul travel affordable to many more people. The -100 series entered service in 1970, and, by the start of the 2000s, those still flying were mainly used as freighters. Pictured on approach to land at LAX, in October 2001, is Boeing 747-146(SF) N702CK c/n 20332 of Kalitta Air. The carrier is based at Willow Run Airport, Detroit, and much of its business is flying parts for the local motor industry. This aircraft was withdrawn from use in 2010.

First flown in October 1970, the -200 variant of the 747 had increased fuel capacity and a stronger airframe. The airline customers had a choice of three engine manufacturers, Pratt & Whitney, Rolls-Royce and General Electric. Arriving at its gate at Bangkok Don Muang International Airport, in February 2001, is Boeing 747-209B B-18255 c/n 21843 of China Airlines which is based in Taipei, Taiwan. This aircraft had a structural failure in May 2002 and broke up in mid-air near Taiwan – all 225 on board died.

British Airways have been one of the largest users of the 747. Pictured at London Heathrow Airport, in February 2000, is Boeing 747-236B G-BDXP c/n 24088. It is in the Landor livery, and this is of note as this scheme had been superseded three years earlier, when the 'World Image' scheme was introduced. This aircraft was sold on, withdrawn from use and broken up in 2010.

Pictured climbing out of Dubai International Airport, in November 2008, is Boeing 747-2B5B(SF) G-MKCA c/n 22482 of MK Airlines, an all-cargo carrier based at Manston, Kent. It ceased operations in April 2010, and this aircraft was put into store in Kemble, UK, before being broken up in 2016.

Turning on to take off on runway 23L at Manchester Airport, in August 2002, is Boeing 747-236B G-BDXJ c/n 21831 of Bournemouth-based European Air Charter. The company ceased operations in December 2010. This aircraft was retired to Dunsfold Aerodrome in 2005 and is used in film productions as a prop.

Moscow-based carrier Transaero Airlines' Boeing 747-219B VP-BQC c/n 22725 is pictured at Manchester Airport in May 2008. The company ceased operations in October 2015. This aircraft was put into store in 2011 and later broken up in Utica–Rome, New York State.

On push back at Nagasaki Airport, in October 2004, is Boeing 747-281B JA8174 c/n 23501 of Tokyo-based ANA (All Nippon Airways). This aircraft was withdrawn from use later that year and put into store at Mojave, California, used in a film and then broken up.

First flown in October 1982, the -300 variant of the 747 featured a stretched upper deck. Seen climbing out of Manchester Airport, in August 2003, is Boeing 747-3H6 B-KAC c/n 23600 of Dragonair Cargo. Based in Hong Kong, in 2006, the company became a wholly owned subsidiary of Cathay Pacific, and in January 2016 it was rebranded as Cathay Dragon. This aircraft was put into store in 2008 and broken up the following year in Victorville, California.

Boeing 747-312 D2-TEA c/n 23410 of Luanda-based TAAG Angola Airlines is pictured at Paris Charles de Gaulle Airport in June 2005. It was broken up at Johannesburg in November 2016, and some parts were used in an aviation-themed bar.

On approach to land at Kansai International Airport, Osaka, in October 2004, is Boeing 747-346 JA8186 c/n 24018, operated by Tokyo-based JALways. It is in the special Reso'cha scheme. The company was owned by JAL and was its charter division. In December 2010, it was merged into the parent company. This aircraft was sold on, operating in Thailand and Nigeria, before eventually being stored in Jakarta.

Whereas the earlier variants of the 747 were gradual improvements, the -400 was a huge leap in performance. The prototype first flew in April 1998 and featured a new 'glass cockpit' with digital avionics. It was flown by a crew of two with no requirement for a flight engineer. A major recognition point was the winglets that help extend the range and reduce fuel burn in long high-altitude cruising. Seen on approach to London Heathrow Airport, in July 2002, is Boeing 747-41R G-VWOW c/n 32745 of Virgin Atlantic Airways. This airframe is now used by another member of the Virgin group, in this case Virgin Galactic, for various test flying duties.

On the move at Paris Charles de Gaulle Airport, in June 2007, is Boeing 747-4B5F HL7462 c/n 26406 of Seoul-based Korean Air Cargo. This aircraft was sold on and now operates for an American company.

Climbing out of San Francisco International Airport, in September 2007, is Boeing 747-4J6 B-2467 c/n 28754 of Beijing-based Air China. This aircraft was put into store in 2014 and broken up the following year at Orlando, Florida.

On the move at Paris Charles de Gaulle Airport, in June 2007, is Boeing 747-428 F-GITH c/n 32868 of French flag carrier Air France. Sold on, this aircraft is now with a company in Iceland.

Pictured, in November 2008, at Dubai International Airport is Boeing 747-422 EP-MNA c/n 24383 in the livery of Blue Sky, an Armenian airline based in Yerevan. The company operated the aircraft for Iranian carrier Mahan Air. Blue Sky ceased operations in 2008, and this aircraft was repainted in full Mahan Air colours and was in store in Tehran at the end of 2021.

On the taxiway at Bangkok Don Muang International Airport, in February 2001, is Boeing 747-4D7 HS-TGJ c/n 24459 of national flag carrier Thai Airways International. It is in the special 'Royal Barge' colours. Sold on, this aircraft now operates for a company in Moldova.

Another special colour scheme is that worn by Boeing 747-481D JA8957 c/n 25642 of ANA (All Nippon Airways). It is in a yellow livery to promote the Pokémon series of video games. It is pictured at Naha Airport, Okinawa, in October 2004 and is a 'Domestic Jumbo'. Japan uses the 747 on internal domestic services with a high-density passenger configuration. This one has 27 business class seats and 542 economy ones. To withstand the shorter routes with far more take-offs and landings than the usual 747, the aircraft have a strengthened undercarriage and structure. Also, they do not have winglets, as these only become effective in long and high cruise situations, not on short trips. This aircraft was withdrawn from use and broken up in Tupelo, Mississippi.

Seen climbing out of San Francisco International Airport, in September 2007, is Boeing 747-422 N199UA c/n 28717 of one of the US's largest carriers, United Airlines. It was withdrawn from use in 2016 in Victorville, California.

On the way to its gate at Bangkok Don Muang International Airport, in January 2002, is Boeing 747-438 VH-OJB c/n 24373 of Sydney-based Qantas (Queensland and Northern Territory Aerial Services). It carries the special 'Aborigine' colour scheme. This aircraft was sold on and later stored in Mojave, California, in 2015.

Pictured at Detroit Metropolitan Airport, in August 2008, is Boeing 747-451 N670US c/n 24225 of Minneapolis-St Paul-based Northwest Airlines. The long-established carrier was taken over and merged into Delta Air Lines, this being completed by early 2010. This aircraft was withdrawn from use in Marana, Arizona, in 2017.

With the perfect name for a Chinese airline, Shanghai-based Great Wall Airlines' Boeing 747-412(BCF) B-2430 c/n 27137 is pictured at Manchester Airport in May 2008. The carrier was merged with China Cargo Airlines in 2011, and this aircraft still serves with it.

Pictured at its Hong Kong Chek Lap Kok Airport base, in March 2003, is Boeing 747-467 B-HOX c/n 24955 of Cathay Pacific Airways. It has special markings named 'Spirit of Hong Kong'. This aircraft was withdrawn from use in October 2012 to be broken up in Kemble, UK.

The 747SP was the 'Special Performance' version. It had several objectives; one was to fill the gap between the 707 and the full-size 747; another was to compete with the Douglas DC-10 and Lockheed L1011 TriStar. It was 48ft (14.63m) shorter than the standard 747 but had a far longer range of nearly 7,000 miles (11,265km). The prototype first flew in July 1975, and just 45 examples were built. Seen on approach to Manchester Airport, in March 2002, is Boeing 747SP-44 F-GTOM c/n 21253 of Paris Orly Airport-based Corsair. This aircraft was withdrawn from use later that year at Chateauroux, and the semi-derelict airframe is used for police training.

First flown in February 1982, the Boeing 757 was the manufacturer's replacement for the best-selling 727, the first jet airliner to pass the 1,000 sales mark. The 757 was the first American airliner to be launched with a foreign engine, this being the British-made Rolls-Royce RB-211-535. Pictured, in August 2007, at Moscow Domodedovo Airport is Boeing 757-230 RA-73008 c/n 25436 of Moscow-based Vim Airlines. The carrier ceased operations in October 2017, and this aircraft was sold on and broken up the following year.

Climbing out of Palma de Mallorca Airport, in September 2000, is Boeing 757-2T7 G-MONE c/n 23293 of Luton-based, UK holiday charter operator Monarch Airlines. The carrier ceased operations in October 2017, whilst this aircraft was converted to a freighter in 2010 and currently operates with an American company.

Boeing 757-2ZO B-2845 c/n 27512, in the livery of Chengdu-based China Southwest Airlines, is pictured at Hong Kong Chek Lap Kok Airport in March 2003. The aircraft had not yet been repainted, as the carrier had been merged into Air China in October of the previous year. Having been converted to a freighter, this aircraft now serves with another Chinese company.

Lining up to take off on runway 23L at Manchester Airport, in August 2002, is Boeing 757-22K EZ-A014 c/n 30863 of Ashkhabad-based Turkmenistan Airlines, the nation's flag carrier. This aircraft still serves with the company.

Seen at its gate, in May 2001, at Amsterdam Schiphol Airport is Boeing 757-230 PH-DBH c/n 24748 of Dutchbird, a holiday charter operator based at the airport. The company ceased operations in December 2004. This aircraft was converted to a freighter in 2011 and currently operates for a US-based company.

Houston-based Continental Airlines' Boeing 757-224(ET) N21108 c/n 27298 is pictured at Manchester Airport in July 2006. The carrier was taken over and merged into United Airlines in March 2011. This aircraft was in store in Roswell, New Mexico, in 2020.

Climbing out of Palma de Mallorca Airport, in September 2000, is Boeing 757-25F G-FCLD c/n 28718 of Manchester-based JMC Air. It had been formed by the merger of Flying Colours and Caledonian Airways, following the purchase by Thomas Cook. The name derives from the son of Thomas Cook, John Mason Cook. It was rebranded Thomas Cook Airlines in March 2003. This aircraft was converted to a freighter and currently operates for a company in India.

Boeing 757-25C B-2849 c/n 27517 of Xiamen Airlines is at Hong Kong Chek Lap Kok Airport in March 2003. This aircraft was put into store in 2015 in the city of Xiamen, the home base of the carrier.

Taking off from runway 09 at Liverpool John Lennon Airport in June 2007 is Boeing 757-28A(ET) G-CEJM c/n 26276 of Flyglobespan. The company had its headquarters in Edinburgh and was declared bankrupt in December 2009. The tail of this aircraft has the name 'Liverpool John Lennon Airport' and a line from his song 'Imagine' – 'Above us only sky' – as well as a drawing he made. In 2014, this aircraft was converted into a freighter and currently operates in India.

Departing Palma de Mallorca Airport, in September 2000, is Boeing 757-2G5 HB-IHR c/n 29379 of Zurich-based Balair. It was a subsidiary of Swissair and operated holiday charter flights. The parent company was declared bankrupt in 2002, and this aircraft was sold on to a UK operator and put into store in Goodyear, Arizona, in 2021.

In the clear blue skies of Vancouver International Airport, in August 2005, Boeing 757-258 C-GMYC c/n 23917, of locally based Harmony Airways, departs. The company used only the titles 'HMY' on the aircraft as an abbreviation for Harmony. The carrier suspended operations in April 2007, and this aircraft was broken up in Greenwood, Mississippi, the same year.

The -300 757 was stretched by 13ft 4in (4.03) forward and 9ft 9in (2.97m) aft of the wing, making it the longest single-aisle airliner. Pictured departing Dubai International Airport, in November 2008, is Boeing 757-330 D-ABON c/n 29023 of Frankfurt-based Condor Flugdienst, a subsidiary of Thomas Cook. It wears a special '50 Year Anniversary' scheme, this aircraft still serves with the holiday charter carrier.

First flown in September 1981, the Boeing 767 was one of the first twin-engine, wide-body jets, and Boeing gave airlines a choice of all three major engine manufacturers. Its main rival was the Airbus A300. Seen at Manchester Airport, in June 2002, is Boeing 767-233(ER) C-GAVC c/n 22527 of Montreal-based Air Canada. This aircraft was withdrawn from use in 2008 and put into store in Roswell, New Mexico.

Pictured on the move at Tokyo Haneda Airport, in October 2004, is Boeing 767-281 JA8251 c/n 23431 of Sapporo-based Air Do Hokkaido International Airlines. The following year, it was converted to a freighter and served with an American operator until 2020. The fuselage was then moved to Wright-Patterson Air Force Base, Ohio, for use as a ground trainer for the KC-46A programme. The KC-46 is the new United States Air Force (USAF) aerial refuelling tanker variant of the 767.

Boeing 767-2B1(ER) XA-OAM c/n 26471 of Mexico City-based Aero Mexico is pictured on the move at Paris Charles de Gaulle Airport in June 2007. This aircraft was put into store in 2014 and broken up two years later in Victorville, California.

Approaching to land at Palma de Mallorca Airport, in September 2000, is Boeing 767-204 G-BOPB c/n 24239 of Luton-based Britannia Airways. The holiday charter carrier was acquired that year by the TUI group of Germany, and, in September 2004, it was rebranded as Thomsonfly. This aircraft was sold on and is currently with an operator in Jordan.

The -300 variant of the 767 first flew in January 1986 and was stretched by 10ft 1in (3.07m) forward and 11ft (3.35m) aft of the wing. Wearing special 'Brazil 500' colours, Boeing 767-341 PP-VOK c/n 24843 of Rio de Janeiro-based VARIG (Viaçao Aérea Rio-Grandense) is at Santiago de Chile Airport in October 2003. The long-established carrier, which dated back to 1927, ceased operations in July 2006. This aircraft was sold on and operated in Poland in 2005. It was withdrawn from use in 2013 and put into store at Durham Tees Valley Airport before being broken up.

On a landing approach to London Heathrow, in July 2002, is Boeing 767-33A(ER) V8-RBL c/n 27189 of Bandar Seri Begawan-based Royal Brunei Airlines, the nation's flag carrier. The aircraft was sold on and operated in Ukraine, and by 2012 it was in store at Kiev (now Kyiv).

Lining up to depart, in August 2003, at Manchester Airport is Boeing 767-38A(ER) G-OOAL c/n 29617 of locally based holiday charter operator Air 2000. The following year, the company was renamed First Choice Airways. This aircraft still operates for a company in the UK.

Boeing 767-34P(ER) B-2490 c/n 33047 of Haikou-based Hainan Airlines is on the move at Dubai International Airport in November 2008. Hainan Island is a Chinese holiday resort. Sold on, this aircraft is currently with an operator in Portugal.

Climbing out of the company base at Santiago de Chile, in October 2003, with the snow-capped Andes Mountains in the background, is Boeing 767-316(ER) CC-CZT c/n 29228 of Lan Chile. The carrier was rebranded as LATAM in 2015, and this aircraft was converted to a freighter in 2020; it is currently with a company in the US.

Boeing 767-338(ER) VH-OGL c/n 25363 of Australian Airlines is pictured, in February 2003, at the company base of Cairns Airport, Queensland. The carrier was a subsidiary of Qantas and operated to locations in Asia with the aircraft in an all-economy 270-seat configuration. Operations ceased in June 2006, and this aircraft was sold on to Canada. It was later converted to a freighter and is currently with a company in the US.

In a very distinctive livery, Boeing 767-328(ER) C-GZMM c/n 27136 of Zoom Airlines prepares to depart Manchester Airport in April 2006. The Ottawa-based carrier ceased operations in August 2008, and this aircraft currently operates for a company in the US.

Hanoi-based Vietnam Airlines is that nation's flag carrier. Seen at Melbourne Tullamarine Airport, in February 2003, is Boeing 767-352(ER) VN-A763 c/n 26261. This aircraft was sold on to several operators, withdrawn from use in 2019 and put into store in Roswell, New Mexico.

Boeing 767-3W0(ER) B-2568 c/n 28148 of Kunming-based China Yunnan Airlines is on the move at Bangkok Don Muang International Airport in February 2001. The carrier was absorbed into China Eastern Airlines during 2004–05. This aircraft was sold on first to a company in Thailand and then to one in America, where it currently serves.

The -400 variant of the 767 was stretched by 11ft 1in (3.38m) forward and 10ft 1in (3.07m) aft of the wing. The prototype first flew in October 1999. Pictured landing at LAX in October 2001, is Boeing 767-432(ER) N833MH c/n 29706 of Atlanta-based Delta Air Lines. This aircraft still serves with the company.

The Boeing Company felt there was a need for an aircraft to fill the gap between the 747 and the 767. As well as this, they had competition from Airbus with the A330 and A340 models, which were more modern in design than the existing Boeing products. The new aircraft was the 777, and it first flew in June 1994; customer airlines had a choice of powerplants from all three leading engine manufacturers. Pictured at Osaka Itami International Airport, in October 2004, is Boeing 777-289 JA009D c/n 27641 of Tokyo-based JAS (Japan Air System). In October 2006, the carrier was taken over and merged into Japan Airlines, and this aircraft was withdrawn from use.

On the move at its base at Ben Gurion International Airport, Tel Aviv, in June 2008, is Boeing 777-258(ER) 4X-ECA c/n 30831 of El Al Israel Airlines, the nation's flag carrier. This aircraft still serves with the company.

Seen during take-off at San Francisco International Airport, in September 2007, is Boeing 777-28E(ER) HL7739 c/n 29175 of Seoul-based Asiana Airlines. This aircraft still serves with the carrier.

Boeing 777-222(ER) VT-AIK c/n 28714 of Air India is at Paris Charles de Gaulle Airport in June 2007. This aircraft was sold on to Russia and later withdrawn from use and stored at Teruel, Spain, in 2015.

The -300 series of the 777 first flew in October 1977, and it was stretched by 17ft 5in (5.3m) forward and 15ft 8in (4.77m) aft of the wing. Climbing out of San Francisco International Airport, in September 2007, is Boeing 777-312(ER) 9V-SWI c/n 34574 of Singapore Airlines. The nation's flag carrier is a large user of the type, with over 50 examples in its fleet, all powered by the Rolls-Royce Trent 892 engine. This aircraft still serves with the company.

Lockheed's TriStar had a difficult start, as the selected powerplant was the Rolls-Royce RB-211. Delays in development, which added to higher costs, brought the engine manufacturer to bankruptcy, and in 1971, the then-Conservative UK government nationalised Rolls-Royce. The prototype TriStar had first flown in November 1970. Pictured at Palma de Mallorca Airport, in September 2000, is Lockheed L-1011 TriStar 1 TF-ABU c/n 1051 of Keflavik-based Air Atlanta Iceland. The carrier was, and still is, a holiday charter operator. This aircraft was equipped with 362 all-economy seats; it was withdrawn and broken up at Helsinge, Sweden, the following year.

Seen at Bangkok Don Muang International Airport, in February 2001, is Lockheed L-1011 TriStar 1 XU-700 c/n 1055 of locally based Angel Airlines. The aircraft was leased from a Cambodian company, hence the registration. The carrier ceased operations in 2003, and this aircraft is in store and derelict in U-Tapao, Thailand.

Montreal-based Air Transat is a current Canadian charter operator. Pictured at Manchester Airport, in June 2002, is Lockheed L-1011 TriStar 500 C-FTSW c/n 1246. The -500 variant was the long-range version, with extra fuel tanks in the centre section. The fuselage was also shortened by 13ft 6in (4.11m) and the wingspan increased by 9ft (2.74m). This aircraft was sold on and operated in several nations. It was in store at Sabha, Libya, in 2012 and is believed to have been destroyed during the on-going civil war.

From the first time it took to the air in 1958, the Douglas DC-8 has proved to be an adaptable aircraft. It was both stretched and re-engined, giving it a service life longer than its rival, the Boeing 707. By the year 2000, most of the DC-8s were either stretched -60 series or re-engined -70 series. Pictured at Minneapolis-St Paul International Airport, in May 2000, is Douglas DC-8-62F N993CF c/n 46028 of Ohio-based Emery Worldwide Airlines, a cargo carrier that ceased operation in August of the following year. The -62 was designed for long-haul operations and was a stretch of 23ft 4in (7.11m) forward and 20ft (6.09m) aft of the wing from the -55 series. This aircraft was sold on to an American carrier, stored in 2009 in Victorville, California, and then broken up.

Pictured crew training at Willow Run Airport, Detroit, in August 2008, is Douglas DC-8-63F N865F c/n 46088 of locally based Murray Air. The company flew a mix of both passenger and freight operations. In December of that year, it was taken over and renamed National Airlines. The -63 variant was an amalgam of the -61 and the -62. It had the longer range of the -62 but the shorter fuselage by 3ft 4in (1.01m), both forward and aft of the wing, of the -61. This aircraft has been preserved at the Yankee Air Museum at Willow Run since 2012.

Seen waiting for its next load of cargo, in September 2007, at Columbus International Airport, Ohio, is Douglas DC-8-71F N715UP c/n 45915 of UPS Airlines, a Louisville-based division of the giant United Parcel Service Company. The -71 variant is a -61 that has been re-engined with the SNECMA/GE CFM-56 turbofan. The engine gave the DC-8 many more years of economic service life. This aircraft was sold on and put into store in 2010 before being broken up.

The first of the short-haul jets were the French Sud Aviation SE-210 Caravelle and the British-made BAC 1-11. Both were well in service before the first American-manufactured Douglas DC-9 took to the air in February 1965. All three had a pair of rear-mounted engines. The original length of the DC-9 was 104ft 5in (31.82m), and the strength of the engineering in its design made it easy for the company to stretch the airframe. Pictured on the move at Minneapolis-St Paul, in May 2000, is Douglas DC-9-14 N8915E c/n 45832 of locally based Northwest Airlines. The carrier was taken over and merged into Delta Air Lines by early 2010. This aircraft was withdrawn from use in 2004 in Marana, Arizona, and broken up.

The -32 DC-9 had a stretch of 15ft (4.57m), a higher maximum take-off weight, and it could be fitted with the higher-thrust versions of the Pratt & Whitney JT8D engine. Seen on approach to LAX, in October 2001, is Douglas DC-9-32 XA-TNT c/n 48113 of Aero California, based at La Paz, Mexico. The carrier ceased operations in July 2008, and this aircraft was put into store.

In April 1967, the Douglas Aircraft Company was taken over by McDonnell Aircraft to form McDonnell Douglas. It was some years before the new company put its name on the DC-9 programme. This became the MD-81, and it first flew in October 1979. The length of the new aircraft was 147ft 10in (45.05m), and it had many updates, including cockpit instrumentation. Pictured landing at Buenos Aires Aeroparque Jorge Newbery, in October 2003, is McDonnell Douglas MD-81 LV-WPY c/n 48024 of the national flag carrier Aerolíneas Argentinas. This aircraft was withdrawn from use in 2007 and broken up the following year.

The MD-82 was designed for operations in hot and high locations. The engines were Pratt & Whitney JT8D-217 turbofans with an output of 20,000lb st. Pictured on the move at Singapore Changi Airport, in February 2003, is McDonnell Douglas MD-82 PK-IMD c/n 49112 of Jakarta-based Bouraq Indonesian Airlines. The carrier ceased operations in July 2005. This aircraft was sold on, and it operated in several countries before being withdrawn from use and broken up.

On the ramp at Cape Town International Airport, in September 2006, is McDonnell Douglas MD-82 ZS-TRE c/n 49387 of Johannesburg-based 1time Airline. The carrier ceased operations in November 2012. This aircraft was sold on and in 2016 was broken up.

Pictured at Naples International Airport, in September 2004, is McDonnell Douglas MD-82 I-DAWT c/n 49210 of Rome-based Alitalia, Italy's national flag carrier. The state-owned airline ceased operations on 15 October 2021 and the same day started services with a new government-owned carrier, ITA Airways. This aircraft was sold on to a company in Africa and later went into store in Uppington, South Africa.

The MD-83 was the same size as the MD-81 but with extra belly tanks, a greater fuel capacity and gross take-off weight. On climb out of Vancouver International Airport, in August 2005, is McDonnell Douglas MD-83 N981AS c/n 53472 of Alaska Airlines. Despite its name, the carrier is based in the city of Seattle. This aircraft was sold on and now operates for a company in Venezuela.

Pictured on the runway at a snowy Luleå Airport, northern Sweden, in April 2005, is McDonnell Douglas MD-83 SE-RDS c/n 49401 of Stockholm-based FlyNordic. In 2007, the carrier was bought by Norwegian Air Shuttle and integrated into its operations. This aircraft was in store in Victorville, California, in 2018.

The MD-90-30 was fitted with a pair of International Aero Engines IAE V2528 turbofans, with an output of 25,000lb st. It had all the improvements of earlier variants, such as a new 'glass cockpit' featuring EFIS (Electronic Flight Information System) and FMS (Flight Management System), that had been introduced in the MD-88. Pictured in its most attractive livery, in October 2004, at Osaka Itami International Airport is McDonnell Douglas MD-90-30 JA001D c/n 53555 of Tokyo-based JAS (Japan Air Systems). The carrier was taken over and merged into Japan Airlines in October 2006. This aircraft was sold on to the US and withdrawn from use in 2019 in San Bernadino, California, and broken up.

A twin-aisle, wide-body airliner powered by a trio of General Electric CF-6 turbofans, the Douglas DC-10 first flew in August 1970. Pictured at Palma de Mallorca Airport, in September 2000, is Douglas DC-10-10 OY-CNT c/n 47833 of Copenhagen-based holiday charter operator Premiair. The carrier was a subsidiary of UK-based Airtours and was rebranded as Thomas Cook Scandinavia in May 2008. This aircraft was sold on in the US and broken up in Bournemouth, UK, in 2005.

The -30 variant of the DC-10 was the long-range version; it had upgraded CF-6-50 engines with an output of 48,000lb st and extra fuel tanks. Because of the extra weight, the -30 had a central undercarriage leg fitted. Seen at Amsterdam Schiphol Airport, in May 2001, is Douglas DC-10-30F N400JR c/n 46976 of DAS Air Cargo, an all-freight company based in Entebbe, Uganda. It ceased operations in September 2007. This aircraft was broken up in Vatry, France, in 2009.

The follow on from the DC-10 was the MD-11; it first flew in January 1990 and was a major update from the earlier model. It now had a new 'glass cockpit' and just two pilots, no flight engineer was required. It was longer by 18ft 6in (5.6m), and the most visible change were the 8ft 9in (2.7m) winglets on an extended wing. The engines were a trio of General Electric CF-6 turbofans with an output of 61,500lb st. Pictured on take-off from Vancouver International Airport, in August 2005, is McDonnell Douglas MD-11 PH-KCH c/n 48562 of Dutch flag carrier KLM. This aircraft was withdrawn from use and broken up in Victorville, California, in 2012.

On pushback at Frankfurt Airport, in June 2001, is McDonnell Douglas MD-11 B-18172 c/n 48469 of Taipei-based Mandarin Airlines. The carrier is a subsidiary of China Airlines. One of the problems with the type was that it initially failed to live up to the range that the manufacturer promised. As a result of this, many operators disposed of their fleets early, and this led to a new role as a very popular freighter. This aircraft was sold on to a US company, converted to a freighter in 2005, and then, in 2014, withdrawn from use and put into store in Victorville, California.

McDonnell Douglas MD-11F B-16113 c/n 48790 of Taipei-based Eva Air Cargo is departing Dubai International Airport in November 2008. This aircraft was later stored and then broken up in San Bernadino, California.

Pictured on the ramp at Ted Stevens Anchorage International Airport, in September 2008, is McDonnell Douglas MD-11F B-2174 c/n 48498 of China Cargo Airlines. Shanghai-based, it is a subsidiary of China Eastern Airlines. This aircraft was sold on to an American operator and later broken up.

Seen at Bangkok Don Muang International Airport, in February 2001, is McDonnell Douglas MD-11 HB-IWG c/n 48452 of Swissair Asia. This company was a subsidiary of Swissair designated to operate services to Taiwan without upsetting the government in Beijing. British Airways and KLM also had similar operations. Zürich-based Swissair ceased operations in April 2002. This aircraft was converted to a freighter in 2006 and serves in the fleet of an American company.

Based in Dallas, Texas, American Airlines is one of the largest carriers in the world. Pictured at London Heathrow, in February 2000, is McDonnell Douglas MD-11 N1761R c/n 48551. The following year, it was sold on and converted to a freighter and is currently with a US-based operator.

Memphis-based Federal Express is one of the giants of the small package delivery service companies. Taking off from Sharjah International Airport, in March 2000, is McDonnell Douglas MD-11F N587FE c/n 48489. This aircraft still serves with the carrier.

The Dutch-built Fokker F.27 Friendship was the most successful, in sales terms, of the late 1950s and early 1960s so-called 'Dakota replacements'. Like the others, the Avro 748, Handley-Page Herald and NAMC YS-11, it was powered by a pair of Rolls-Royce Dart turboprops. The first F.27 flew in November 1955 and entered service with Aer Lingus in 1958. Pictured, in March 2000, at an unusually wet Sharjah International Airport is Fokker F.27 Friendship 200 AP-BCZ c/n 10305 of PIA (Pakistan International Airlines). This aircraft has since been broken up.

First flown in December 1985, the Fokker 50 was the manufacturer's attempt to bring the F.27 design up to date. It had new Pratt & Whitney PW124 turboprops with an output of 2,160shp, a longer nose and new cockpit instrumentation. Seen at Nagoya Airport, in October 2004, is Fokker 50 JA8200 c/n 20307 of locally based NAL (Naka Nihon Air Line Service). The carrier was renamed Air Central in February the following year. This aircraft is now in service with a company in the Philippines.

Climbing out of Palma de Mallorca Airport, in September 2000, is Fokker 50 EC-GKV c/n 20274 of Valencia-based Air Nostrum. This aircraft was sold on to a carrier in Iran (see next picture).

Pictured at take-off at Dubai International Airport, in November 2008, is Fokker 50 EP-LCB c/n 20274 of Kish Island-based Kish Air. This aircraft is still in Iran, albeit with another carrier.

As well as producing the F.27, Fokker also went into the short-haul jet market with the F.28 Fellowship. It first flew in May 1967, and the powerplants were a pair of rear mounted Rolls-Royce Spey turbofans. Arriving at Cairns Airport, Queensland, in February 2003, is Fokker F.28 Fellowship 4000 P2-AND c/n 11118 of Port Moresby-based Air Nuigini, the flag carrier for Papua New Guinea. This aircraft was sold on to a carrier in Africa and later broken up in Lanseria, South Africa, in 2012.

This Fokker F.28 Fellowship 1000 LV-LZN c/n 11048 is operated in the colours of two carriers – LAER (Lineas Aéreas Entre Rios) and American Falcon. It is pictured at Buenos Aires Aeroparque Jorge Newbery in October 2003. Neither of the airlines still operate, and this aircraft joined the Argentine Air Force.

To update the F.28, Fokker produced two different jets, the Fokker 70 and 100; both were powered by a pair of new fuel-efficient Rolls-Royce Tay 620 turbofans with an output of 13,850lb st. On the flightdeck, new electronic instruments were fitted. Lining up to take off at Manchester Airport, in April 2004, is Fokker 70 PH-KZM c/n 11561 of KLM Cityhopper. Based in Amsterdam, it is a subsidiary of KLM and operates regional services. This aircraft now operates for a company in Cyprus.

The Fokker 100 was 15ft 2in (4.62m) longer than the F70. Seen at Zürich Airport, in September 2004, is Fokker 100 HB-JVD c/n 11498 of locally based Helvetic Airways, in a most distinctive colour scheme. This aircraft now operates for a company in Nigeria.

On the move at Brisbane Airport, in February 2003, is Fokker 100 VH-FWI c/n 11318 of locally based Alliance Airlines. The company still operates this aircraft.

Brazil's Embraer company (Empresa Brasileira de Aerońautica SA) was formed in 1969 and has grown to be a major aircraft manufacturer of commuter-size turboprop and smaller airliners. Its first design was the EMB 110 Bandeirante, which first flew in August 1972 and sold just short of 500 examples. Seen at Montevideo Carrasco International Airport, in October 2003, is Embraer EMB 110P1 Bandeirante CX-MAS c/n 110393 of locally based Aeromás. This aircraft still serves with the Uruguayan carrier.

The next design from Embraer was the Brasilia, a 30-seat commuter airliner powered by a pair of Pratt & Whitney PW115 turboprops with an output of 1,500shp. The prototype first flew in July 1983. Pictured at Moscow Zhukovsky International Airport, in August 2007, is Embraer EMB-120 Brasilia N203SW (now RA-02856) c/n 120240 of Moscow Vnukovo-based Atlant-Soyuz Airlines. The carrier ceased operations in 2011, and this aircraft is now in store.

Embraer EMB-120ER Brasilia N215SW c/n 120281 of Utah-based Skywest Airlines is on the move at San Francisco International Airport in September 2007. The carrier usually operates in the livery of other airlines that it flies commuter services for. This aircraft was sold on and is now serving with a company in Angola.

The first jet airliner from Embraer was the 50-seat EMB-145. It first flew in August 1995 and was powered by a pair of rear-mounted Allison AE3007A turbofans with an output of 7,040lb st. Pictured at Manchester Airport, in August 2002, is Embraer RJ-145EP SE-DZD c/n 145185 of Skyways Express, which is based at Linkoping, Sweden. The carrier ceased operations in May 2012, and this aircraft was sold on to the US and later put into store.

A 37-seat version of the EMB-145 was created by shortening the fuselage by 11ft 7in (3.54m); this was known as the EMB-135, and it entered service in 1999. Seen at Paris Charles de Gaulle, in June 2005, is Embraer RJ-135LR F-GYPE c/n 145492 of Le Puy-Lourdes-based Hex'Air. The extra titles are to advertise the Savoie area of France. In January 2017, the carrier was merged with Twin Jet, and this aircraft still serves with the company.

First flying in February 2002, the Embraer 170 was one of the newest airline types to be seen during the decade. It was 98ft 1in (29.9m) long and powered by a pair of General Electric CF-34-8E turbofans with an output of 14,200lb st, and it could seat up to 76 passengers. Pictured at Manchester Airport, in July 2006, is Embraer 170STD OH-LEK c/n 17000127 of Helsinki-based Finnair. This aircraft was withdrawn from use, stored at Kemble in 2016 and then broken up.

On the move at Dubai International Airport, in November 2008, is Embraer 170LR HZ-AEO c/n 17000161 of Jeddah-based Saudi Arabian Airlines, that nation's flag carrier. This aircraft was withdrawn from use in 2016 and stored at the company base.

The Embraer 190 was stretched to be 118ft 11in (36.25m) long, and the powerplants were now rated at 18,500lb st. The prototype first flew in March 2004. Pictured at Washington Dulles International Airport, in October 2006, is Embraer 190AR N236JB c/n 19000035 of New York-based JetBlue Airways. The company was the launch customer for the type. This aircraft still serves with the carrier.

The longest variant of the new Embraer jet is the 195. It first flew in December 2004 and is 126ft 10in (38.66m) long. Pictured on approach to Manchester Airport, in May 2008, is Embraer 195LR G-FBEK c/n 19000168 of Exeter-based Flybe. It was the first to operate the version, starting in September 2006. The carrier ceased operations in March 2020, and a new company plans to launch using the same name during 2022. This aircraft is in store at Norwich, UK.

At the present time, it is very unlikely that any decade of future aviation operations will not feature a Dakota. Many aircraft have been designed, built, marketed and operated as the so-called 'Dakota replacement', but history has proved that the only true replacement for a Dakota is another Dakota. Pictured, in May 2000, at Palmer Municipal Airport, Alaska, is Douglas DC-3 Dakota N50CM c/n 13445 of locally based Woods Air Service. The carrier suspended operations in October of that year, and this aircraft was broken up.

To fly in an aircraft that is over 80 years old is not to everyone's taste. However, across the world, passengers are happy to pay to experience the early days of commercial aviation. Pictured at Melbourne Essendon Airport, in February 2003, is Douglas DC-3 Dakota VH-TMQ c/n 32884 of appropriately named Air Nostalgia. The carrier is based at this location and still operates the aircraft.

Based in Canada's Northwest Territories, Buffalo Airways have become TV stars with a programme about the carrier's operations in that harsh environment and the staff who run the airline. Pictured, in September 2008, at Hay River Airport, NWT, is Douglas DC-3 Dakota C-GPNR c/n 13333. Hay River is, alongside Yellowknife, one of the main operating bases. The DC-3 has one engine running at the passenger's request, so they could get pictures of the engine start before climbing on board to fly back to Yellowknife. This aircraft is still operated by the company.

Seen on take-off at Coventry Airport, UK, in May 2003, is Douglas DC-3 Dakota G-AMRA c/n 26735 of locally based Air Atlantique. The company ceased operations in 2008, and this aircraft was sold on to a company in Germany, where it still operates.

The Douglas Aircraft Company itself produced its own 'Dakota replacement', with a DC-3 fuselage extended by 3ft 3in (0.99m) to add seating capacity, a new vertical tail added and the horizontal tail plane and wingtips squared off. The engine nacelles were redesigned to allow the retracted undercarriage to be fully enclosed. The final touches were new engines in the form of a pair of Wright Cyclone R-1820 air-cooled radial pistons with an output of 1,475hp. In this new guise as the Super DC-3, it first flew in June 1949 but failed to sell to the airlines, with just three being built for Capital Airways. A small number of others were converted from existing DC-3 airframes. There was, of course, nothing wrong with the design, there were just too many ex-military C-47/DC-3 airframes available at far cheaper prices than new built ones. The type was saved by an order for 100 from the United States Navy under the designation R4D-8 (C-117 from 1962). Douglas Super DC-3S N30TN c/n 43159 of Anchorage-based TransNorthern is pictured at Kenai, Alaska, in September 2008. This aircraft still serves with the company but suffered minor damage, in August 2021, when the right-hand undercarriage collapsed upon landing at Goodnews, Alaska.

The number of the Douglas Aircraft Company's four-engine piston-powered transports in operation by the start of the decade was very low. Pictured at Harry Mwanga Nkumbula International Airport, Livingstone, Zambia, in September 2006, is Douglas DC-4 Skymaster ZS-AUA c/n 42934 of Rovos Air. The Pretoria, South Africa-based company was a division of Rovos Rail Tours. It was configured for passengers and had brought tourists to view the nearby Victoria Falls. The carrier ceased operations in 2014, and this aircraft is now preserved at Rand Airport at the South African Airways Museum.

The more usual load for a DC-4 by this decade was either cargo or, in this case, bulk fuel for remote settlements or mining camps. In September 2008, at Fairbanks International Airport, with all four Pratt & Whitney R-2000 Twin Wasp air-cooled radial pistons running, is Douglas DC-4 Skymaster N3054V c/n 10547 of locally based Brooks Fuels. The company ceased operations, and this aircraft is currently with another carrier in the state.

Douglas DC-4 Skymaster VH-PAF c/n 27352 is pictured, in February 2003, at Brisbane Archerfield Airport. It was owned by Pacific Air Freighters, which was based at that location. The carrier ceased operations later that year. This aircraft is now preserved with Australia's Historic Aircraft Restoration Society at Illawara, New South Wales, and wears period Qantas livery on one side and a Trans Australian Airlines one on the other.

First flying in June 1945, the DC-6 was the second of the four-engine Douglas designs to enter service. It was powered by 2,100hp Pratt & Whitney R-2800 Double Wasp radials. Seen, in May 2000, on approach to Ted Stevens Anchorage International Airport is Douglas DC-6BF N867TA c/n 45202 of locally based NAC (Northern Air Cargo). This aircraft had been converted, in April 1968, by Sabena at Brussels, to have a swing tail for ease of loading long items – note the bulges for the hinges on the rear fuselage. It was withdrawn from use and then broken up.

Douglas DC-6BF N151 c/n 45496 of Fairbanks-based Everts Air Cargo is on the ramp, in September 2008, at Ted Stevens Anchorage International Airport. The company sold this aircraft, and in 2020 it flew to its new home at Sola Airport, Stavanger, Norway, to be preserved in the livery of Braathens SAFE, the airline that had once operated this airframe in the 1960s for holiday charter flights.

Pictured in temporary storage at Kenai, Alaska, in September 2008, is Douglas DC-6A N500UA c/n 44597 of Universal Airlines, which was based in Victoria, Texas. Its role in the largest state of the US was the seasonal carriage of fish to the 'lower 48' states. This aircraft was sold on to another company in America.

Seen flying at its Coventry Airport base, in May 2003, is Douglas DC-6A G-APSA c/n 45497 of Air Atlantique. The company ceased operations in 2008, and this aircraft was transported, by road, to the South Wales Aviation Museum in St Athan in 2021 for preservation in British Eagle livery.

The Curtiss Commando can now only be found in the remote parts of Canada or Alaska. Albeit the same layout as the Dakota, this aircraft is much larger. Power came from a pair of 2,000hp Pratt & Whitney R-2800 radial pistons. Pictured being pushed out of its hangar, in September 2008, at Yellowknife Airport, is Curtiss C-46A Commando C-GTXW c/n 30386 of Buffalo Airways. This aircraft was written off in a landing accident at Déline, NWT, in September 2015.

Curtiss C-46F Commando C-GIBX c/n 22472 of First Nations Transportation is seen, in September 2008, at its Gimli, Manitoba, base. Transport Canada, the government licensing body, suspended the carrier's operating certificate in April the following year, and this aircraft was withdrawn from use.

Pictured at its Fairbanks International Airport base, in May 2000, is Curtiss C-46F Commando N1822M c/n 22521 of Everts Air Fuels. As the company name suggests, Its role is the delivery of bulk fuel to remote locations around the state of Alaska. This aircraft, named *Salmon Ella*, was substantially damaged during a landing accident at Manley Hot Springs Airport in July 2018. So valuable and almost irreplaceable in its role was this aircraft, that it was taken back to Fairbanks for repair.

One of the first military freighters to have a ventral rear loading ramp that allowed vehicles to drive straight into the hold, the Antonov An-8 was powered by a pair of Ivchenko AI-20 turboprops. By the start of the 1990s, it was thought that they had all been retired, but, with the break-up of the USSR, they began to be seen in Africa and the Middle East. Pictured under maintenance, in March 2000, is Antonov An-8 3C-DDA c/n OB-3430 in the markings of Mandala Air Cargo. This aircraft, registered in Equatorial Guinea and seen here at Sharjah, was broken up at Fujairah, UAE. In 2004, Antonov withdrew the certificate of airworthiness and support, bringing to an end the legal operations of the type.

Registered in São Tomé and Príncipe, Antonov An-12BP S9-SAM c/n 3341408 of Sharjah-based British Gulf International is on the move at Dubai International Airport in November 2008. The An-12 was first flown in December 1957 and was, and still is, the standard military freighter for communist and non-aligned nation's air forces. Power was provided by four 4,000shp Kuznetsov NK-4 turboprops, with later versions having Ivchenko AI-20A engines. In 2009, the UAE put a ban on An-12 operations, and the carrier closed down its operations. Prior to this, in January 2009, this aircraft was damaged beyond economic repair at its Sharjah base, when on take-off the left-hand undercarriage failed and one of the propellers struck the runway.

Antonov An-12 EL-ALJ c/n 8346202 of Sharjah-based Santa Cruz Imperial Airlines is seen, in March 2000, at the company base. The carrier suspended operations in 2008, and this aircraft was broken up here the same year.

In the USSR, the aircraft designers were also looking to replace their old piston engined airliners. These were the Ilyushin IL-14 and the Lisunov Li-2; this latter aircraft was a licence-built version of the DC-3. The Antonov OKB (Design Bureau) in Kiev (now Kyiv) produced the An-24, powered by a pair of 2,550shp Ivchenko IA-24V turboprops. It first flew in December 1962. Pictured at Moscow Vnukovo International Airport, in August 2007, is Antonov An-24RV UR-BXC c/n 37308902 of Motor Sich Airlines, which is based at Zaporozhye, Ukraine. This aircraft still serves with the company.

Seen on the ramp, in August 2007, at Moscow Vnukovo International Airport is Antonov An-24B RA-47289 c/n 07306509 of Khanty-Mansiysk-based UTair Aviation. This aircraft still serves with the company.

The An-26 was the cargo version of the An-24 and had a rear-loading ramp with drive-in capability. On the move at Lima Jorge Chávez International Airport, in October 2003, is Antonov An-26B-100 OB-1778-P c/n 14205 of locally based ATSA (Aero Transport SA). This aircraft was sold on and now serves with a carrier in Ukraine.

Taxiing to runway 27 at Liverpool John Lennon Airport, in May 2004, is Antonov An-26B SP-FDO c/n 10503 of Katowice-based Exin Co. Such operations into Liverpool usually brought parts for local car factories. This aircraft was written off in March 2010 in a landing accident at Tallinn, Estonia. With one failed engine, it landed on a frozen lake and then sank through the ice after stopping.

The Antonov An-124 is a very large civil and military freighter powered by four Lotarev D-18T turbofans with an output of 51,590lb st. It has captured a large slice of the civil market as it has the ability to move outsized or very heavy loads. It is the only aircraft that can be hired for these jobs. Pictured on approach to Osaka Kansai International Airport, in October 2004, is Antonov An-124-100 Ruslan RA-82043 c/n 9773054155101 of Ulyanovsk-based Volga-Dnepr Airlines. This aircraft still serves with the company.

The Yak-40 was a regional airliner that could seat up to 32 passengers. First flown in October 1966, it was powered by a trio of rear-mounted 3,300lb st Ivchenko AI-25 turbofans. Pictured at Moscow Bykovo Airport, in August 2007, is Yakovlev Yak-40 RA-88274 c/n 9721253 of locally based Bylina, a private and business charter company. This aircraft was put into store in 2012.

The Yak-42 first flew in March 1975 and was a medium-range airliner. Power came from three rear-mounted Ivchenko D-36 turbofans with an output of 14,325lb st. Climbing out of Moscow Domodedovo Airport, in August 2007, is Yakovlev Yak-42D RA-42374 c/n 4520423914340 of Kazan-based Tatarstan Air. In December 2013, its licence to operate was revoked and all services were suspended. This aircraft had gone into store in 2011.

With the undercarriage nearly retracted, Yakovlev Yak-42D EP-QFB c/n 452042203019 of Fars Air Qeshm based at Qeshm Island, Iran, takes off from Dubai International Airport in November 2008. The carrier ceased operations in 2021, and prior to that this aircraft had been put into store in 2013.

Heading for its gate at Frankfurt Airport, in June 2001, is Yakovlev Yak-42D T9-ABD c/n 4520422016201 of Sarajevo-based Air Bosna. The carrier ceased operations in July 2015. This aircraft was sold on to a company in Ukraine in 2007. Later, it was withdrawn from use and broken up in 2014.

Pictured at Moscow Bykovo Airport, in August 2007, is Yakovlev Yak-42D RA-42346 c/n 4520423708311 of Nalchik-based Elbrusavia. The carrier's licence to operate was revoked in April 2009. This aircraft was put into store in 2008 and broken up at Moscow in 2017.

Russia's IL-18 had a much longer front-line service life than its western contemporaries, the Lockheed Electra and the Bristol Britannia. In the West, passengers wanted pure jets – and got them – whilst in the USSR, 'customer choice' were not words that Aeroflot understood. Powered by four turboprops, the IL-18 first took to the air in July 1957. Seen on the ramp, at its Sharjah International Airport base, in March 2000, is Ilyushin IL-18V 3C-KKJ c/n 184006903 of Air Cess. The following year, the carrier changed its name to Air Bas, and this aircraft, registered in Equatorial Guinea, was sold on to a carrier in Kazakhstan and later withdrawn from use.

Wearing the identities of two carriers at Sharjah International Airport, in March 2000, is Ilyushin IL-18D EX-75442 c/n 187009702, owned by locally based Phoenix Aviation, but registered in Kyrgyzstan. It has the name Sudan Airways on the rear fuselage and the logo on the nose. Sudan Airways is that country's flag carrier, whilst Phoenix was rebranded as Ave.com. This aircraft was sold on to a company in the Democratic Republic of the Congo in 2003 and later withdrawn from use and broken up in 2007.

A long-range airliner with four rear-mounted engines, the IL-62 first flew in January 1961. The 'M' variant had extra fuel tanks in the fin and Soloviev D-30KU turbofans. Pictured at the company base of Moscow Domodedovo Airport, in August 2007, is Ilyushin IL-62M RA-86575 c/n 1647928 of Interavia Airlines. In October the following year, the carrier suspended services. This aircraft was withdrawn from use in 2009 and broken up at this location in 2012.

Pictured at Sharjah International Airport, in March 2000, is Ilyushin IL-62M XU-229 c/n 4445032 of Yana Airlines, based at Phnom Penh, Cambodia. The carrier was renamed Mekong Airlines, and this aircraft was broken up in 2006.

First flown in March 1971, the IL-76 is one of the most widely used and versatile cargo aircraft. It is powered by four Soloviev D-30KP turbofans with an output of 26,455lb st. Seen on the ramp at Sharjah International Airport, in March 2000, is Ilyushin IL-76TD EP-ALE c/n 0043453575 of Tehran-based Atlas Air. The carrier suspended operations in 2002, and this aircraft is currently with a company in Sudan.

Pictured on the ramp at Moscow Domodedovo Airport, in August 2007, is Ilyushin IL-76TD RA-76357 c/n 1023414467 of Alrosa, which is based in Mirny in the Republic of Sakha-Yakutia. This aircraft was withdrawn from use and used as a spares source; by 2017, two engines were missing.

On the ramp at Sharjah International Airport, in March 2000, is Ilyushin IL-76MD UR-76629 c/n 0053458745 of Kiev (now Kyiv)-based ATI Aircompany. The carrier ceased operations in 2002. This aircraft joined the Ukrainian Air Force and was later withdrawn and broken up.

The first Soviet wide-body airliner, the IL-86 first took to the air in December 1976. It was powered by four Samara NK-86 turbofans with an output of 29,320lb st but was, however, quite underpowered. Wearing a most attractive livery on the ramp at Sharjah International Airport, in March 2000, is Ilyushin IL-86 EK-86118 c/n 51483209086 of Yerevan-based Armenian Airlines. The carrier ceased operations in 2003, and this aircraft was withdrawn from use and broken up in 2015.

Ilyushin IL-86 UK-86056 c/n 51483203023 of Tashkent-based Uzbekistan Airways, the nation's current flag carrier, is seen, in March 2000, at Sharjah International Airport. This aircraft was withdrawn and broken up at the company base.

The IL-96 was the manufacturer's answer to the underpowered IL-86. It had more powerful Aviadvigatel PS-90A turbofans with an output of 23,275lb st, a new wing with winglets fitted, and the overall length of the fuselage was reduced by 29ft 3in (8.91m). Pictured at Moscow Sheremetyevo International Airport, in August 2007, is Ilyushin IL-96-300 RA-96005 c/n 74393201002 of the state carrier Aeroflot Russian Airlines. This aircraft was withdrawn from use in 2014 at this location, the carrier's base, and used as a fire trainer.

A short-haul airliner powered by a pair of rear-mounted Soloviev D-30 turbofans with an output of 14,990lb st, the Tu-134 first flew in July 1963. Seen on the ramp at Moscow Vnukovo International Airport, in August 2007, is Tupolev Tu-134A RA-65903 c/n 63750 of Rusline. The carrier is still based at this location, but this aircraft was withdrawn from use in 2011 and broken up the following year.

Tupolev Tu-134A-3 RA-65096 c/n 60257 is pictured, in August 2007, at Moscow Sheremetyevo International Airport. It is in the smart livery of Arkhangelsk-based Aeroflot Nord. The carrier was 51 per cent owned by Aeroflot and was its second regional airline. In 2009, it was renamed Nordavia. This aircraft was withdrawn from use.

On the ramp at Moscow Domodedovo Airport, in August 2007, is Tupolev Tu-134B-3 RA-65694 c/n 63235, operated by Kras Air (Krasnoyarsk Airlines). It was a member of the AiRUnion alliance, an amalgam of five airlines, hence the titles on the fuselage. Kras Air ceased operations in October 2008. This aircraft was withdrawn from use and preserved at the Aviapark Shopping Mall, on what used to be Khodynka Airport, Moscow. In October 2020, it was moved to a private airfield at Oreshkovo.

A medium-range airliner powered by a trio of rear-mounted Kuznetsov NK-8 turbofans, the Tu-154 first flew in October 1968. It was one of the most widely used of all the airliners from the USSR, and into the first decade of the 2000s it was a common sight around Russia and the new republics, as well as at the Western European airports they operated at. Pictured at Moscow Domodedovo Airport, in August 2007, is Tupolev Tu-154B-2 4K-474 c/n 474 of Turan Air, which was based at Baku, Azerbaijan. The carrier ceased operations in 2013, and this aircraft went into store.

Tupolev Tu-154B-2 EY-85466 c/n 466 of Dushanbe-based Tajikistan Airlines is seen at Sharjah International Airport in March 2000. This aircraft was withdrawn from use in 2007 and broken up the following year.

Pictured on the ramp at Moscow Vnukovo International Airport, in August 2007, is Tupolev Tu-154M RA-85630 c/n 759 of Makhachkala-based Daghestan Airlines. The Republic of Daghestan is situated within Russia in the north Caucasus of Eastern Europe, along the Caspian Sea. The carrier ceased operations in December 2011, and this aircraft was put into store.

Seen heading to its gate at Frankfurt Airport, in June 2001, is Tupolev Tu-154M EW-85706 c/n 881 of Belavia Belarusian Airlines. The Minsk-based carrier is still current, but this aircraft was withdrawn from use in 2009 at the company base and broken up.

On lease from Russian carrier Kolavia is Tupolev Tu-154M RA-85784 c/n 968. Pictured at Dubai International Airport, in November 2008, it carries the name of Taban Air, an airline based in the Iranian city of Masshad. This aircraft later returned to Kolavia.

Left: On the move at Frankfurt Airport, in June 2001, is Tupolev Tu-154M RA-85697 c/n 870 of Novosibirsk-based Sibir Airlines. In 2005, the Siberian carrier was rebranded as S7. This aircraft was withdrawn from use in 2008 and broken up in 2013.

Below: Parked up with the engines covered at a snowy Salzburg W. A. Mozart Airport, in January 2006, is Tupolev Tu-154M RA-85833 c/n 1020 of Ural Airlines. The Ekaterinburg-based carrier now operates Airbus types. This aircraft was sold on and is now in store.

On the ramp at Moscow Domodedovo Airport, in August 2007, is Tupolev Tu-154M RA-85723 c/n 905 of Samara Airlines. The carrier was based in the city of the same name, and it ceased operations in September 2008, as it was part of the AiRUnion group. This aircraft was withdrawn from use and put into store.

Right: Lined up to take off at Manchester Airport, in June 2002, is Tupolev Tu-154M LZ-HMI c/n 706 of Sofia-based Hemus Air, in the operating livery of Balkan Holidays. The company ceased operations in 2014 when it merged with Bulgarian Air. This aircraft was sold on to a company in Russia then one in Iran and later put into store.

Below: On the move at Frankfurt Airport, in June 2001, is Tupolev Tu-154M RA-85694 c/n 867 of Kras Air. The carrier was based in the city of Krasnoyarsk and ceased operations in October 2008. This aircraft was withdrawn from use and then broken up.

Pictured a long way from its home base in the far east of Russia, in August 2007, is Tupolev Tu-154M RA-85766 c/n 923 of Vladivostok Avia. In November 2011, Aeroflot took a majority stake in the company, and operations using the city name were ended, in December 2013, when it joined with SAT Airlines to form Aurora. This aircraft was put into store at its base in 2009.

Left: Seen landing at Palma de Mallorca Airport, in September 2000, is Tupolev Tu-154M OM-AAA c/n 1014 of Slovenske Slovak Airlines. The Bratislava-based carrier ceased operations in February 2007, and this aircraft was sold on to a carrier in Russia, withdrawn from use in 2009 and broken up in 2013 in St Petersburg.

Below: Tupolev Tu-154M EP-CPG c/n 748 of Tehran-based Caspian Airlines is pictured at Dubai International Airport in November 2008. This aircraft was written off in July the following year on a flight from Tehran to Armenia, when, shortly after take-off, it impacted into terrain, killing all 168 people on board.

Seen on the move at Frankfurt Airport, in June 2001, is Tupolev Tu-154M LZ-LCA c/n 829 of Sofia-based Bulgarian Air Charter. In May 2021, the carrier was rebranded as European Air Charter. This aircraft was withdrawn from use and broken up.

Right: On the taxiway at Moscow Sheremetyevo International Airport, in August 2007, is Tupolev Tu-154M RA-85204 c/n 886 of Rossiya, which is based in St Petersburg. This aircraft was withdrawn from use and broken up.

Below: On its way to its gate at Frankfurt Airport, in June 2001, is Tupolev Tu-154M RA-85658 c/n 808 of St Petersburg-based Pulkovo Aviation Enterprise. In October 2006, the company merged with Rossiya and adopted its name. This aircraft was sold on to another Russian company, withdrawn from use in 2011 and broken up in Norilsk, Russia, in 2018.

Tupolev Tu-154M RA-85700 c/n 875 is on the move at Moscow Vnukovo International Airport in August 2007. It is operated by Yakutia Air, based in the city of Yakutsk in the Republic of Sakha-Yakutia, one of the more remote areas in that vast nation. This aircraft was withdrawn from use and broken up.

The Tu-204 was designed to replace the large numbers of Tu-154s in service in the USSR and satellite countries. It first flew in January 1989 and was powered by a pair of Perm PS-90A turbofans with an output of 35,589lb st. It became a victim of dates. By the time all the test flying was completed, the political map of the region had changed – the USSR no longer existed, and the many new airlines that formed could buy or lease Western-built aircraft, and so sales were low. Pictured at Moscow Zhukovsky International Airport, in August 2007, is Tupolev Tu-204-100E CU-T1701 c/n 14507464035 of Cubana de Aviation, Cuba's flag carrier. This aircraft was withdrawn from use at its Havana base in 2016.

Tupolev Tu-204-100 RA-64022 c/n 1450743164022 of KMV (Kavkazskie Mineralnye Vody) is at Moscow Vnukovo International Airport in August 2007. Based in the city of Mineralnye Vody, the carrier ceased operations in October 2011, and this aircraft was withdrawn from use.

The Antonov An-24 was licence built in China as the Xian Y-7; it was then developed into the MA-60, 'MA' standing for 'Modern Ark' and the '60' for the maximum seating capacity. The prototype first took to the air in March 2000 and was certified in June the same year. It had a lot of Western-designed equipment, the largest being a pair of Pratt & Whitney Canada PW127J turboprops with an output of 2,750shp each. AVIC 1 MA-60 Z-WPK c/n 0303 of Harare-based Air Zimbabwe is pictured at Johannesburg O. R. Tambo International Airport in September 2006. The change from Xian to AVIC in the name relates to the political change of placing the Aviation Industries of China in control of the airframe, engine and component manufacturers. This aircraft was withdrawn from use at the carrier's base and used as a spares source.

First flown in August 1963, the British Aircraft Corporation's BAC 1-11 was a short-haul jet liner with a pair of rear-mounted Rolls-Royce Spey turbofans. It accumulated a large order book, including major American carriers. By the start of the 2000s, few were still in service, mainly because of noise restrictions. Pictured at Paris Charles de Gaulle Airport, in June 2007, is BAC 1-11-488GH YR-HRS c/n 259 of Bucharest-based MIA Airlines. The carrier specialised in VIP charter work, and this aircraft was equipped with 19 seats. The company ceased operations in 2011, and the aircraft was sold on to Mali.

Derived from the Challenger business jet, the (Bombardier) Canadair CRJ (Regional Jet) had been stretched to a length of 87ft 10in (26.77m) and could carry 50 passengers. Power was from a pair of rear-mounted General Electric CF-34 turbojets. It first flew in May 1991. On the move at Osaka Itami International Airport, in October 2004, is Canadair CRJ-100ER JA01RJ c/n 7052 of Sendai-based Fair Inc. The carrier changed its name to IBEX Airlines that month. This aircraft was withdrawn from use in 2014 and is in store at Stockholm.

Canadair CRJ-200LR OE-LSC c/n 7299 of Styrian Spirit, which was based in Graz, Austria, is on the move at Zürich Airport in September 2004. The carrier ceased operations in March 2006, and this aircraft was sold on to a company in Canada. The CRJ-200 had up-rated engines and a longer range.

Canadair stretched the -200 to make the -700; it was 18ft 3in (5.56m) longer and could seat up to 78 passengers. It kept the same powerplants but with higher thrust. Pictured climbing out of Vancouver International Airport, in August 2005, is Canadair CRJ-700ER C-FDJZ c/n 15049 of Air Canada Jazz, which operates regional services for the main company. This aircraft still serves with the carrier.

The CRJ-900 was yet another stretch of the fuselage, this one being 12ft 10in (3.91m) with a seating capacity of up to 90 passengers. Seen at Berlin Tegel Airport, in May 2008, is Canadair CRJ-900ER EI-DRK c/n 15076 of Rome-based Air One CityLiner. In April 2011, it was rebranded as Alitalia CityLiner. This aircraft was sold on and now operates in America.

First flown in September 1981, the British Aerospace 146 was a short-haul airliner powered by four Lycoming (later Allied Signal) ALF 502 turbofans, it was one of the quietest aircraft in service. Pictured, in September 2006, at Brno-Tuřany Airport, Czech Republic, is BAe 146-200(QT) EC-FZE c/n E2105 of Madrid-based Pan Air Lineas Aéreas, a sister company of TNT Airways. The carrier ceased operations in May 2016. The 'QT' stood for 'Quiet Trader' and was the windowless cargo version. It was sold on to an operator in Australia and still serves with it.

BAe146-200A VH-YAE c/n E2107 of QantasLink is pictured at Melbourne Tullamarine Airport in February 2003. Sydney-based, the carrier operates services for Qantas. This aircraft was sold on and withdrawn from use at Adelaide and broken up in September 2015.

The -300 variant of the 146 was the longest and was stretched 8ft 1in (2.46m) forward and 7ft 8in (2.33m) aft of the wing. It first flew in May 1987. Seen on approach to land at London Stansted Airport, in August 2003, is BAe 146-300 G-UKAC c/n E3142 of locally based Buzz. The low-cost carrier had been formed by KLM and was sold to Ryanair in January 2003. Operations ceased in October 2004. This aircraft was withdrawn from use in Cologne. In 2018, Ryanair restarted a Polish-based airline using the Buzz name.

BAe 146-300 G-JEBG c/n E3209 of Exeter-based Flybe is pictured at Manchester Airport in May 2008. It is in a special colour scheme to advertise online casino company Mansion.com. Flybe ceased operations in March 2020, and a company was launched using the same name in 2022. This aircraft was sold on to a company in Malta, withdrawn from use in 2009 and then broken up in 2014.

Following new developments with the interior, and avionics and powerplant improvements, the BAe 146-300 was rebranded as the Avro RJ100. On the taxiway at Frankfurt Airport, in June 2001, is Avro RJ 100 OO-DWI c/n E3342, operated by DAT (Delta Air Transport), a subsidiary of Sabena. The carrier flew regional services for the Belgian flag carrier with aircraft in Sabena livery. Following the November 2001 collapse of Sabena, it became, in 2002, SN Brussels Airline and later Brussels Airline. This aircraft was withdrawn from use and broken up in Cranfield in 2017.

Pictured against the blue sky at Palma de Mallorca Airport, in September 2000, is Avro RJ100 G-BXAR c/n E3298 of BA CityFlyer Express. Gatwick-based, it was a subsidiary of British Airways and operated a franchise agreement in its colours. This aircraft still has one of the 'World Image' tails, 'Delftblue Daybreak', a Dutch design by Hugo Kaagman. It is based upon Delft traditional ceramic designs. These images did linger for some time due to the cost of repainting an aircraft before a scheduled service. This aircraft was damaged on landing at London City Airport, in February 2009, when the nose wheel collapsed causing extensive damage to the equipment bay. It was deemed a write-off.

The Lockheed Hercules has been in an unbroken production run since 1954, albeit with many updates over the years. It is the transport backbone of many of the air forces of the world. The company also produced a civil version for bulk cargo operators. Seen at Yellowknife Airport, in September 2008, is Lockheed L-100-30 Hercules C-GUSI c/n 4600 of First Air. The company merged with Canadian North in November 2019, and this aircraft was sold on to an operator in America.

Lockheed L-100-30 Hercules N401LC c/n 4606 of Lynden Air Cargo is on the ramp at the company base of Ted Stevens Anchorage International Airport in September 2008. This aircraft is still in service with the company.

Operating the only airworthy C-133 Cargomaster in the world was Ted Stevens Anchorage International Airport-based Cargomaster Corporation. The ex-USAF bulk transport was limited to federal or state contracts only. Pictured, in May 2000, at the company base, is Douglas C-133A Cargomaster N199AB c/n 45164. The carrier suspended operations the following year. In August 2008, this aircraft was flown to Travis Air Force Base Museum, California, for preservation.

First flown in 1957, the Lockheed Electra was powered by four Allison 501 turboprops with an output of 3,750shp. It had a short front-line life, as the ticket-buying public wanted pure jets, but it did have a long life with smaller carriers and still serves as a cargo carrier to this day. On approach to Ted Stevens Anchorage International Airport, in May 2000, is Lockheed L-188C Electra N1968R c/n 2007 of locally based Reeve Aleutian Airways. The carrier ceased operations in December of that year, and this aircraft was sold on to Canada and converted to the role of a water bomber and is still operating as such.

Lockheed L-188C(F) C-GLBA c/n 1145 of Buffalo Airways is pictured outside the company hangar, in September 2008, at its Yellowknife main operating base. This aircraft is currently in store in Red Deer, Alberta, for Buffalo Airways.

As well as normal cargo operations, one of the roles Coventry-based Atlantic Airlines was tasked with was from the British government for oil slick dispersal. The aircraft would have spray bars attached, and the dispersant liquid would be in a removable tank inside the fuselage. Pictured, in May 2003, is Lockheed L-188C(F) Electra G-LOFE c/n 1144, demonstrating this role at the company base. In October 2008, the company was renamed West Atlantic UK, and this aircraft was sold on to a company in Canada where it still operates.

The fitting of Allison 501 turboprops, with an output of 3,750shp, to Convair 340 and 440 airframes gave the aircraft a whole new lease of life that extends to this day. Pictured, in May 2000, at Ted Stevens Anchorage International Airport, is Convair 580 N538JA c/n 34 of ERA Aviation. The '580' was the new designation for the Allison-powered aircraft. This aircraft was configured for passenger operations and could seat 48 in an all-economy layout. ERA ceased operations in February 2009, and this aircraft had been sold on to a company in Canada for spare parts in 2003.

The Avro (later Hawker Siddeley) 748 was the most successful of the British-built 'Dakota replacements'. It first flew in June 1960 and was powered by a pair of Rolls-Royce Dart turboprops. Seen at Fairbanks International Airport, in May 2000, is Hawker Siddeley HS748-276 Srs.2A C-FAGI c/n 1699 of Air North, which is based at Whitehorse, Yukon. The company withdraw this aircraft from service in December 2020, and it is in store at its base.

To bring the 748 up to date, Hawker Siddeley (now known as British Aerospace) produced the ATP or Advanced Turboprop. It first flew in August 1986 and was 16ft 6in (5.03m) longer than the 748. The vertical fin was a different shape and the wingspan increased. The new engines were a pair of Pratt & Whitney PW124A turboprops with an output of 2,653shp. Pictured at Manchester Airport, in June 2002, is BAe ATP G-MANC c/n 2054 of Isle of Man-based Manx Airlines. The carrier ceased operations in August of that year, and this aircraft was sold on and eventually broken up in Coventry in 2018.

Climbing out of Palma de Mallorca Airport, in September 2000, is BAe ATP EC-GSE c/n 2038 of locally based Air Europa Express, a sister company of Air Europa. This aircraft was sold on, converted to a freighter and currently operates in Sweden.

After a gap of 30 years, the well-known Swedish military aircraft manufacturer Saab returned to the civil market with the 340. It could seat up to 35 passengers and first flew in January 1983. Power came from a pair of General Electric GE CT7s with an output of 1,630shp. Pictured at Manchester Airport, in August 2002, is Saab SF340A G-RUNG c/n 340A-086 of Aurigny Air Services, which is based on the Channel Island of Guernsey. Sold on, this aircraft now operates in Guatemala.

Saab SF340B N251CJ c/n 340B-251 of Colgan Air, based at Manassas, Virginia, is seen on the move at Washington Dulles International Airport in October 2006. The regional carrier ceased operations in September 2012, and this aircraft was withdrawn from use and put into store.

Saab stretched the 340 by 23ft 11in (7.28m) to produce the 2000. It could now seat up to 50 passengers. The prototype first took to the air in March 1992, and the new type was powered by a pair of Allison AE2100A turboprops with an output of 4,125shp. Pictured at Moscow Zhukovsky International Airport, in August 2007, is Saab 2000 VP-BPR c/n 2000-061 of Voronezh-based Polet Flight. The carrier ceased operations in December 2014, and this aircraft returned to Saab. It is currently in store at Linköping.

British Aerospace developed the Jetstream from the original Handley Page HP-137 following its demise. Built at Prestwick, Scotland, the first aircraft flew in March 1980 and was powered by a pair of Garrett TPE331 turboprops with an output of 1,200shp. It could carry 19 passengers. Seen on the move at Buenos Aires Aeroparque Jorge Newbery, in October 2003, is BAe 3201 Jetstream 32EP LV-ZST c/n 941 of Cordoba-based Aerovip. The carrier ceased operations in 2004, restarted in 2009 and finally closed in November of the following year. This aircraft was sold on to a company in Colombia.

The Jetstream 41 was longer by 8ft 3in (2.51m) forward and 7ft 9in (2.36m) aft of the wing. The Garrett turboprops now produced 1,500shp, and the seating was for 29 passengers. The prototype first flew in September 1991. Pictured ready to depart Manchester Airport, in April 2004, is BAe 4100 Jetstream 41 G-MAJF c/n 41008 of Humberside-based Eastern Airways. This aircraft was withdrawn from use and broken up.

BAe 4100 Jetstream 41 OY-SVS c/n 41014 of Billund-based SUN-AIR of Scandinavia is about to depart Manchester Airport in August 2002. The carrier operates a franchise to fly service for British Airways, hence the colours scheme. It does, however, have SUN-AIR in small letters on the nose. The aircraft has one of the 'World Image' liveries, in this case the one designed by Martha Masanabo of the Ndebele people of South Africa. It was sold on first to a company in the UK, then to one in Sweden and then withdrawn from use.

The Metroliner was a 19-seat commuter aircraft jointly developed by the Fairchild and Swearingen Aircraft companies. It was powered by a pair of Garrett TPE331 turboprops. Pictured at Brisbane Archerfield, in February 2003, is Swearingen SA227AC Metro III VH-UZS c/n AC-616 of Townsville-based Macair Airlines. The carrier ceased operations in January 2009, and this aircraft now operates in Canada.

Swearingen SA227AC Metro III N41NE c/n AC-741B of Ted Stevens Anchorage International Airport-based Pen Air is seen at its home base. The carrier ceased operations in April 2020, and this aircraft was sold on to a company in Canada.

Developed from the box-like SC-7 Skyvan, Short Brothers of Belfast produced the SD330. It was a small transport aircraft with a passenger capacity of 30, powered by a pair of Pratt & Whitney Canada PT-6A turboprops. The prototype first flew in August 1974. Pictured on the ramp at Columbus International Airport, Ohio, in September 2007, is Short SD330-200 N2629P c/n SH3079, operated by Air Cargo Carriers. The Milwaukee-based company still operates, but this aircraft has been withdrawn from service.

Shorts followed the 330 with the 360, which was longer, had a single fin and could carry up to 36 passengers. The PT-6A engine had an output of 1,327shp. Its first flight was in June 1981. Pictured at Brisbane Airport, in February 2003, is Short SD360-300 VH-SEG c/n SH3760 of Sunshine Express Airlines. The carrier is based at Maroochydore, Queensland. This aircraft was sold on and now operates in Denmark.

Climbing out of Vancouver International Airport, in August 2005, is Short SD360-200 C-GPCW c/n SH3622 of locally based Pacific Coastal Airlines. This aircraft was sold on and now operates in the US.

First flown in March 1981, the Dornier 228 was a 19-seat commuter airliner powered by a pair of 776shp Garrett TPE331-5 turboprops. Pictured in its hangar at Yellowknife Airport, in September 2008, is Dornier Do228-202 C-FPSA c/n 8122 of locally based Summit Air Charters. This aircraft is still operated by the company.

Dornier followed the 228 with the 328, which first flew in December 1991. It could seat up to 32 passengers and was powered by a pair of Pratt & Whitney PW119B turboprops. Seen on approach to land at Grand Canyon National Park Airport, in September 2007, is Dornier Do328-100 N330MX of North Las Vegas Airport-based Vision Airlines. The carrier ceased operations in May 2017, and this aircraft was withdrawn from use.

To overcome some of the comments Dornier received from airlines whilst trying to sell the Do328, it decided to redevelop it into a jet. The turboprops were replaced with a pair of Pratt & Whitney Canada PW306B turbofans. In 1996, Dornier was taken over by Fairchild Aircraft, and, as Fairchild Dornier, it continued the development of what was now known as the Do328JET. Pictured at Manchester Airport, in May 2007, is Fairchild Dornier Do328JET OY-NCM c/n 3190 of SUN-AIR of Scandinavia. The Billund-based company operates as a franchise for British Airways and still operates this aircraft.

ATR (Avions de Transport Régional) was a joint company set up by France's Aérospatiale and Italy's Aeritalia in 1981. Its role was to build a twin-engine turboprop for regional services. The result of this was the ATR-42, the number 42 being its seating capacity. The prototype first flew in August 1984, and the power came from a pair of Pratt & Whitney Canada PW120 turboprops with an output of 1,800shp. Seen on the move, in September 2006, at Cape Town International Airport, is ATR-42-500 A2-ABP c/n 512 of Gaborone-based Air Botswana, that nation's flag carrier. This aircraft was sold on and broken up at Toulouse in 2019.

Pictured on the ramp at Moscow Zhukovsky International Airport, in August 2007, is ATR-42-500 4K-AZ52 c/n 667 of Azal Azerbaijan Airlines. The carrier is based in Baku, and this aircraft was sold on and now operates in Indonesia.

The ATR-72 was a follow-on design from the -42. It was longer by 14ft 9in (4.49m) and had an extended wingspan of 8ft 1in (2.45m). The '-72' was the seating capacity, but each airline would fix its own seat pitch. Power for the new type came in a pair of Pratt & Whitney Canada PW124B turboprops with an output of 2,160shp. On the move at Bangkok Don Muang International Airport, in February 2001, is ATR-72-202 RDPL-34132 c/n 396 of Lao Aviation. The carrier is based in the capital Vientiane. Sold on, this aircraft was converted to a freighter in 2011 and currently operates in Switzerland.

On push back from its gate at Bangkok Don Muang International Airport, in January 2002, is ATR-72-201 HS-TRA c/n 164 of locally based national flag carrier Thai Airways International. This aircraft was sold on and is in store in Thailand.

On the move at Kraków John Paul II International Airport, in June 2008, is ATR-72-202 SP-LFH c/n 478 of Eurolot. Based in Warsaw, the company was a subsidiary of the national flag carrier LOT Polish Airlines, and it operated both domestic and nearby international services. Owing to financial difficulties, the company ceased operations in March 2015. This aircraft was damaged beyond economic repair at Warsaw in July 2011, when, whilst on the ground, it was struck by a vehicle with baggage carts, which ran into the still-running number two engine.

Few would have expected that an aircraft that first entered production in 1937 would have still be in production in 1969. However, this was the case for the Beechcraft model 18, usually just referred to as the Beech 18. Examples can still be found in service to this day, mostly fitted with floats for use in Canada and Alaska, where large numbers of lakes abound. Pictured at Campbell River Harbour Airport (seaplane base, SPB), in September 2008, is Beech 18 C-FGNR c/n CA-191 of Vancouver Island Air. The carrier is based at that location, and this aircraft still serves with it.

The Beechcraft 1900 Airliner was a 19-seat commuter that first flew in September 1982. The powerplants were a pair of 1,100shp Pratt & Whitney Canada PT-6A-65B turboprops. Seen at Oxnard, California, in October 2001, is Beech 1900C Airliner N330AF c/n UB-38 of Dallas-based Ameriflight, a small package cargo operator. This aircraft still serves with this carrier.

Despite the almost identical designation, the Beech 1900D is vastly different from the 'C' model. The newer variant had the cabin volume expanded by 28.5 per cent and winglets fitted, as well as ventral strakes to increase directional stability. The engines were now rated at 1,279shp, and the prototype first flew in March 1990. Seen awaiting its next set of passengers at Grand Canyon National Park Airport, in May 2009, is Beech 1900D Airliner N567MA c/n UE-067 of Las Vegas-based Maverick Airlines. This aircraft was sold on and is now in store.

The Cessna Caravan was first flown in December 1982 and has sold worldwide as a 14-seat commuter, cargo carrier or a mixture of both. Power is from a single 675shp Pratt & Whitney Canada PT-6A turboprop. Pictured in its hangar at Asunción Silvio Pettirossi International Airport, Paraguay, in October 2003, is Cessna 208A Caravan I ZP-CAR c/n 208-00033. It is operated by TAM (Transportes Aéreos del Mercosur). The carrier is now known as LATAM Paraguay, and this aircraft was sold on and now operates in the US.

The Caravan can be used as a floatplane just as well as with land operations. On the move at Yellowknife Water Aerodrome (SPB), in September 2008, is Cessna 208 Caravan C-GATY c/n 208-00305 of Air Tindi. The carrier is based at Yellowknife, and this aircraft still serves with it.

Small aircraft still hold an important place in the world of commercial aviation. One of the most versatile has been the Canadian-built Beaver. The prototype first flew in August 1947, and the type can and does operate on wheels, skis or floats. A single 450hp Pratt & Whitney Wasp Junior radial piston engine powers the aircraft. Pictured about to land, in August 2005, at Vancouver Harbour Flight Centre (SPB) is de Havilland Canada DHC-2 Beaver 1 C-GFDI c/n 606 of Nanaimo SPB-based Baxter Aviation. The carrier was taken over by West Coast Air in April 2007, and this aircraft still operates in Canada.

To extend the life and the operating costs, many Beavers have been re-engined with a turboprop, usually a Pratt & Whitney Canada PT-6. Since this unit is much lighter than the piston one it replaced, the fuselage is extended to maintain the centre of gravity. Pictured in August 2005 at its base at Vancouver International Water Airport (the airport's SPB) is de Havilland DHC-2 Turbo Beaver III C-FDHC c/n 1677TB45 of Seair Seaplanes. The aircraft is still owned by the company.

Following on from the Beaver came the Otter, and it first flew in December 1951. The original aircraft were all powered by a 600hp Wasp R-1340 radial piston, but most Otters flying today have been re-engined with the PT-6A turboprop. Seen at Lake Hood SPB Anchorage, In September 2008, is de Havilland Canada DHC-3 Turbo Otter N2899J c/n 425 of Rust's Flying Service. The carrier is based at this location, and the aircraft still serves with it.

De Havilland Canada are famous for the short take-off and landing performance of the aircraft it designs and builds. Since it first flew in May 1965, the Twin Otter powered by a pair of PT-6A turboprops has operated worldwide on wheels, skis and floats. Pictured at Monument Valley Airport, Utah, in May 2009, is de Havilland Canada DHC-6 Twin Otter Vista Liner 300 N173GC c/n 295 of Grand Canyon Airlines. As can be seen, the windows of the Vista Liner are extra large for viewing sites of natural beauty, such as the Grand Canyon. This aircraft still serves with the company.

First taking to the air in June 1983, Canada's Dash-8 has had a long life because of the aircraft's ability to be stretched and re-engined. Pictured at Vancouver International Airport, in August 2005, is de Havilland Canada DHC-8-102 Dash-8 C-FDNG c/n 166 of Hawkair Aviation Services, which is based at Terrace, British Colombia. The company suspended operations in November 2016, and this aircraft was sold on and still operates in Canada.

On tow at Naha Airport, Okinawa, in October 2004, is de Havilland Canada DHC-8-103 Dash-8 JA8974 c/n 540 of RAC (Ryukyu Air Commuter). The carrier is owned by Japan Transocean Air and is based at this location. This aircraft was sold on and currently operates in Norway.

On the move at Nagasaki Airport, in October 2004, is de Havilland Canada DHC-8-201 Dash-8 JA801B c/n 566 of Oriental Air Bridge. The company is based at this location, and this aircraft still serves with it.

First flown in January 1998, the Dash-8-400 series took the length up to 107ft 9in (32.8m) from the original -100 series length of 73ft (22.25m). The new engines were 5,071shp Pratt & Whitney PW150A turboprops. Lining up to take off at Manchester Airport, in July 2004, is de Havilland Canada DHC-8-402 Q400 LN-WDC c/n 4071 of Bodo-based Widerøe, one of the largest regional carriers in Scandinavia. This aircraft was sold on and now operates in the Philippines.

Seen approaching its gate at Osaka Itami International Airport, in October 2004, is de Havilland Canada DHC-8-402 Q400 JA842A c/n 4082, operated by A-net Air Nippon Network. Based in Sapporo, the carrier merged and was rebranded as ANA Wings in October 2010. This aircraft is still with the company.

First flown in June 1965, the Britten-Norman Islander is a very versatile aircraft, with simple systems and is powered by a pair of 260hp Lycoming piston engines. The aircraft could seat up to ten passengers. Pictured at Sde Tieman Airport, Israel, in June 2008, is Britten-Norman BN-2A Islander 4X-AYS c/n 376 of Beersheba-based Ayeet Aviation. This aircraft was withdrawn from service and broken up.

The Piper Navajo has been used as an executive aircraft, commuter feed-liner and small parcel carrier in worldwide locations. It first flew in September 1964 and was powered by a pair of 300hp Lycoming piston engines. Pictured ready to go at Tobalaba Eulogio Sánchez Airport, Chile, in October 2003, is Piper PA-31 Navajo CC-CFK c/n 31-607 of Lassa Linea de Aeroservicios. The company is based at this location. This aircraft was destroyed in August 2006, when it crashed in northern Chile. Both people on board died.

Having established parity with Boeing, the Airbus consortium went on to surpass its rival with aircraft across the whole range of sizes. Smallest of all the Airbus range was the A318. It first flew in January 2002 and was shorter than the A319 by 2ft 7in (0.79m) ahead and 5ft 3in (1.6m) aft of the wing. It also had the tallest fin and shortest wingspan of all the A320 family of aircraft. Pictured on approach to Manchester Airport, in April 2007, is Airbus A318-111 F-GUGP c/n 2967 of Paris-based Air France. The French carrier has the aircraft configured with 123 all-economy seats, and, whilst the company still operates this aircraft, it is in the process of replacing them with the Airbus A220.

The first airline to put the A318 into service was Denver-based Frontier Airlines, when it started operations with them in July 2003. It equipped its fleet with 118-seat interiors. Seen on the move at San Diego International Airport, in October 2006, is Airbus A318-111 N802FR c/n 1991. All aircraft of the fleet have an animal or bird on the fin, in this case an elk. This aircraft was withdrawn from service in 2013 and broken up in St Athan, UK. Airbus no longer produce the A318 (it built 80 examples in total), as it would now compete with the A220 model.

First flying in August 1991, the A319 was, for some years, the smallest Airbus, being 5ft 3in (1.6m) forward and 7ft (2.13m) aft of the wing shorter than the original base line A320. Pictured at Dubai International Airport, in November 2008, is Airbus A319-112 A9C-EU c/n 1884 of the Bahrain-based flag carrier Gulf Air. Sold on, this aircraft now operates in Spain.

Airbus A319-113 EI-DVD c/n 647 is seen at Paris Charles de Gaulle in June 2007. It was operated by Wind Jet, based at Catania, Italy. The carrier ceased operations in August 2012, and this aircraft was sold on to a company in Nigeria before being withdrawn from use in 2018 and stored at Lagos.

Climbing out of Vancouver International Airport, in August 2005, is Airbus A319-112 N925MX c/n 1925 of Mexico City-based Mexicana. The carrier ceased operations in August 2010, and this aircraft was sold on and operated in several countries before it was withdrawn from use and broken up in Goodyear, Arizona, in 2019.

Pictured at its gate at Orlando International Airport, in April 2005, is Airbus A319-132 N811BR c/n 2431 of Dulles-based low-cost carrier Independence Air. January the following year saw the end of operations. This aircraft currently operates in China.

Heading for its gate at Berlin Tegel Airport, in May 2008, is Airbus A319-112 D-ABGH c/n 3245 of locally based Air Berlin. The company ceased operations in October 2017, and this aircraft is currently with another German carrier.

About to line up to depart on runway 27 at Liverpool John Lennon Airport, in May 2004, is Airbus A319-111 HB-JZB c/n 2043 of easyJet Switzerland. Based in Geneva, it is an associate company of UK-based easyJet. Sold on, this aircraft now operates for a carrier in Spain.

The first of the Airbus single-aisle models was the A320. The prototype first took to the air in February 1987, and the whole range are now the best-selling jet airliners to date. Pictured at Bangkok Don Muang International Airport, in January 2002, is Airbus A320-321 VT-EPO c/n 80 of Delhi-based Indian Airlines. This carrier had a special version of the A320, in that it had a four-wheel main undercarriage leg rather than the usual two-wheel one. This was to solve problems caused by the poor state of some of the runways the company operated from. Its route network was mainly domestic, with some regional international services. This option is no longer available to airline customers. Government-owned, the airline was merged into Air India in July 2007, and this aircraft was preserved as a restaurant at Mohri, Ambala.

On approach to Palma de Mallorca Airport, in September 2000, is Airbus A320-214 G-VKID c/n 1130 of Gatwick-based Virgin Sun. The carrier was a member of the Virgin Group and ceased operations in October of the following year. This aircraft is currently in operation in the US.

Airbus A320-212 PH-VAE c/n 579 of Maastricht-based V-Bird Netherlands Airlines is lining up to take off at Manchester Airport in April 2004. January the following year saw the carrier cease operations. This aircraft was sold on first to a company in Germany and then to one in Bahrain (see next picture).

Seen climbing out of Dubai International Airport, in November 2008, is Airbus A320-212 A9C-BAY c/n 579 of Bahrain Air. The carrier ceased operations in February 2013. This aircraft (the same airframe as the V-Bird) was sold on to an operator in Ukraine, and then later withdrawn from use and broken up in Goodyear, Arizona, in 2015.

Airbus A320-212 I-PEKW c/n 814 of Milan-based Volareweb.com is pictured at Naples International Airport in September 2004. The company was merged into Alitalia in February 2015, and this aircraft was sold on and currently operates in Jordan.

Tripoli, Libya-based Afriqiyah Airways Airbus A320-231 S5-AAB c/n 113 is at Paris Charles de Gaulle in June 2007. It has a Slovenian registration and was sold on and withdrawn from service in Tucson, Arizona, in 2019.

Pictured at Hong Kong Chek Lap Kok Airport, in March 2003, is Airbus A320-214 B-2206 c/n 986 of Xian-based China Northwest Airlines. The previous year, the company had been merged into China Eastern Airlines, but it had not yet been repainted. This aircraft was sold on and withdrawn from use in 2020.

On the ramp at Macau International Airport, in February 2003, is Airbus A320-232 B-MAH c/n 805 of locally based Air Macau. Sold on, this aircraft now operates in Aruba.

Airbus A320-214 9K-CAE c/n 3016 of Jazzera Airways, which is based in Kuwait City, is seen at Dubai International Airport in November 2008. This aircraft was sold on and put into store in Greensboro, North Carolina.

Climbing out of runway 09 at Liverpool John Lennon Airport, in June 2007, is Airbus A320-232 HA-LPK c/n 3143 of fast-growing, Budapest-based Wizz Air. This aircraft still serves with the company.

Heading for its gate at Frankfurt Airport, in June 2001, is Airbus A320-211 F-OHGC c/n 407 of Amman-based flag carrier Royal Jordanian. Sold on, this aircraft now operates in Iran.

Departing from Palma de Mallorca Airport, in September 2000, is Airbus A320-214 F-GRSH c/n 749 of Paris-based Star Airlines. In November 2006, the carrier's name was changed to XL Airways. This aircraft was sold on to a company in Italy and later withdrawn from use and broken up in Goodyear, Arizona, in 2015.

With the background of the pure blue sky of Palma de Mallorca, in September 2000, Airbus A320-214 HB-IHX c/n 942 of Edelweiss Air takes off. Zürich-based, the carrier is a holiday charter operator and still operates this aircraft.

Airbus A320-232 N453UA c/n 1001 of Ted Airlines is pictured at Orlando International Airport, in April 2005. Chicago-based, it was a low-cost, low-fare division of United Airlines. It ceased operations in January 2009, and this aircraft still operates in America.

On the move to its gate at Berlin Tegel Airport, in May 2008, is Airbus A320-211 EC-ICR c/n 240 of Clickair. The Barcelona-based carrier was merged with Vueling in July the following year. This aircraft was withdrawn from use and broken up in Kemble, UK, in 2013.

Pictured at Seattle-Tacoma International Airport, in June 2009, is Airbus A320-214 N634VA c/n 3359 of San Francisco-based Virgin America. In April 2018, the carrier was taken over and merged into Alaska Airlines. This aircraft was withdrawn from use in 2019 and broken up two years later in Marana, Arizona.

Seen at a wet Amsterdam Schiphol Airport, in June 2007, is Airbus A320-214 D-AXLC c/n 1564 of locally based Martinair. The company is a subsidiary of KLM and is now an all-cargo carrier. This leased aircraft, hence the German registration, was sold on to a company in Colombia and then put into store in Greenwood, Mississippi, in 2020.

Airbus A320-211 EK32008 c/n 229 is pictured at Dubai International Airport in November 2008. It was operated by Yerevan-based Armavia. The carrier ceased operations in March 2013, and this aircraft serves on with another airline in Armenia.

The longest of the single-aisle Airbus range is the A321. The fuselage was stretched by 14ft (4.26m) forward and 8ft 9in (2.66m) aft of the wing. The prototype first flew in March 1993. On the ramp at Macau International Airport, in February 2003, is Airbus A321 B-22606 c/n 731 of Taipei-based Trans Asia Airways. The carrier ceased operations in March 2016, and this aircraft was withdrawn from use to be broken up at Goodyear, Arizona, in 2016.

Pictured at its gate at Amsterdam Schiphol Airport, in May 2001, is Airbus A321-211 EI-CPD c/n 841 of Dublin-based Irish flag carrier Aer Lingus. This aircraft was sold on to a company in Russia and has since been broken up.

Ready to take off at Manchester Airport, in July 2006, is Airbus A321-211 G-NIKO c/n 1250 of locally based MyTravel Airways. The holiday charter operator was renamed Thomas Cook Airlines in 2008. This aircraft was converted into a freighter in 2021 and is currently with a UK company.

The first Airbus design to fly, the A300, first flew in October 1972. This was a wide-body, twin-engine, twin-aisle airliner that could seat over 300 passengers. Pictured climbing out of Palma de Mallorca Airport, in September 2000, is Airbus A300B4-120 OY-CNL c/n 128 of Premiair. The Copenhagen-based holiday charter operator was a division of the UK's Airtours. It was rebranded as MyTravel Airways in 2002 and Thomas Cook Airlines Scandinavia in 2008. This aircraft was sold on to an operator in Turkey and later put into store.

Lined up ready to depart Manchester Airport, in June 2002, is Airbus A300B4-203FF G-SWJW c/n 302 of locally based Air Scandic International Aviation. The carrier ceased operations in 2005, and this aircraft was sold on to an operator in Iran, withdrawn from use and put into store in 2016.

Seen at its departure gate at Bangkok Don Muang International Airport, in January 2002, is Airbus A300B4-103 EP-MHE c/n 035 of Mahan Air, which is based at Kerman, Iran. This aircraft is preserved at the company base as a cabin trainer.

Airbus A300B4-203(F) EP-ICF c/n 173 of Tehran-based Iran Air Cargo is pictured at Dubai International Airport in November 2008. This aircraft was withdrawn from use and put into store at the company base in 2014.

Pictured at Sharjah International Airport, in March 2000, is Airbus A300B4-203(F) G-CEXH c/n 117 of Bournemouth-based Channel Express. The all-cargo company were rebranded as the holiday charter company Jet2 in January 2006. This aircraft was sold on to a Turkish company and later broken up.

The -600 series of the A300 was a complete update of the design. It had a new 'glass cockpit', was stretched by 21in (53.34cm), had a longer range, and now just had a flight crew of two; the role of flight engineer was no longer needed thanks to the new instrument layout. On tow at Hong Kong Chek Lap Kok Airport, in March 2003, is Airbus A300-605R B-2325 c/n 746 of Shanghai-based China Eastern Airlines. This aircraft was converted into a freighter in 2016 and still operates in China.

On the move at Bangkok Don Muang International Airport, in February 2001, is Airbus A300-622R B-2323 c/n 739 on lease to locally based Thai company Angel Airlines. The company ceased operations in 2003. This aircraft was converted to a freighter and currently operates in Turkey.

First flown in April 1982, the A310 was the second Airbus design to enter service. It was shorter than the A300 by 22ft 8in (6.9m) and had a smaller wing area. It did, however, have a much longer range, with the -300 version able to fly 5,000 miles (8,047km). Seen arriving at a damp Frankfurt Airport, in June 2001, is Airbus A310-325(ET) F-OHPR c/n 702 of Sana'a-based Yemenia. This aircraft was withdrawn from use in 2013 and put into store.

Pictured at Dubai International Airport, in November 2008, is Airbus A310-308 9K-ALC c/n 663 of Kuwait Airways, that nation's flag carrier. This aircraft was withdrawn from use in Roswell, New Mexico, in 2016.

Airbus A310-304(ET) CS-TEX c/n 565 of Lisbon-based TAP Air Portugal. It is at Paris Charles de Gaulle Airport in June 2007. Sold on, this aircraft now operates in Iran.

Seen upon arrival at Manchester Airport, in April 2002, is Airbus A310-304 TC-JCY c/n 478 of Istanbul-based THY Turkish Airlines. In 2008, the company had this aircraft converted to a freighter for its cargo operations and then withdrew it from use in 2015.

S7 Airlines, based at Novosibirsk, Siberia, has one of the most distinctive colour schemes of any carrier today. Seen at Dubai International Airport, in November 2008, is Airbus A310-204 VP-BLT c/n 486. This aircraft was withdrawn from use and went into store in Amman, Jordan, in 2009.

Approaching to land at London Heathrow Airport, in July 2002, is Airbus A310-222 3B-STJ c/n 350 of Beirut-based MEA (Middle East Airlines). This Mauritius-registered aircraft was withdrawn from use and stored the following year in Greenwood, Mississippi, and later broken up.

Lined up to take off at Manchester Airport, in August 2003, is Airbus A310-203 TC-JYK c/n 172 operated by KTHY (Kıbrıs Türk Hava Yolları). Its base was in Ercan in Northern Cyprus, a state only recognised by Turkey. It was a subsidiary of Turkish Airlines and ceased all operations in June 2010. This aircraft went into store at Istanbul in 2004 and was later broken up.

Airbus produced two new designs, both were derived from the A300; they were the A330 and A340. The two had the same fuselage cross-section as the A300 and the new pair had the same basic fuselage and wing design. Also new were fly-by-wire, side stick controls and a cockpit with an EFIS. The A330 was twin-engined and designed for medium- to long-haul routes, while the A340 had four engines for long-haul services. The A330 first flew in November 1992. Photographed from the balcony at Berlin Tegel Airport, in May 2008, is Airbus A330-223 D-ALPA c/n 403 of LTU (Lufttransport Unternehmen). The Düsseldorf-based carrier was bought by Air Berlin in 2007, and it stopped using the brand name in 2009. This aircraft was sold on to a company in the UK and in 2020 was stored in Düsseldorf.

On the move at Manchester Airport, in April 2001, is Airbus A330-323 N672UW c/n 333 of US Airways, one of the largest carriers in the country. In 2015, the company was taken over and merged into American Airlines. This aircraft was put into store in Roswell, New Mexico, in 2020.

Pictured approaching to land at Manchester Airport, in March 2002, is Airbus A330-243 G-WWBB c/n 404 of East Midlands-based British Midland Airways. In October 2012, the carrier was merged into British Airways. This aircraft was sold on, operated in several nations and put into store in 2020.

Showing off its smart new livery at Dubai International Airport, in November 2008, is Airbus A330-321 HS-TEH c/n 122 of Bangkok-based Thai Airways International, the nation's flag carrier. This aircraft was withdrawn from use in 2015.

Lined up to take off at Manchester Airport, in July 2006, is Airbus A330-302 A7-AED c/n 680 of Doha-based Qatar Airways. This aircraft has special livery to advertise the '15th Asian Games 2006'. It still serves the carrier.

Pictured at Manchester Airport, in July 2006, is Airbus A330-243 A6-EYG c/n 724 of Abu Dhabi-based Etihad Airways. This aircraft still serves the company.

Seen ready to depart Manchester Airport, in April 2004, is Airbus A330-243 G-OJMB c/n 427 of locally based Thomas Cook Airlines. The company ceased operations in September 2019, and this aircraft was sold on to a Canadian company and later put into store in Marana, Arizona, in 2020.

The A340 first flew in October 1991. Pictured at Paris Charles de Gaulle Airport, in June 2007, is Airbus A340-313 F-OJTN c/n 395, operated by Papeete-based Air Tahiti Nui. This aircraft was withdrawn from use in 2018 and later broken up at San Bernadino, California.

Seen on push back from its gate at Frankfurt Airport, in June 2001, is Airbus A340-211 D-AIBF c/n 006 of German flag carrier Lufthansa. This aircraft was sold on to a company in South Africa, withdrawn from use in Lourdes, France, in 2014 and later broken up.

Pictured on approach to London Heathrow Airport, in July 2002, is Airbus A340-313X 6Y-JMM c/n 216 of Kingston-based Air Jamaica. The carrier ceased operations in 2015. This aircraft was sold on and operated by several companies before being withdrawn from use in 2014 and broken up in Goodyear, Arizona.

The A340-500 first flew in February 2002 and was designed to fly ultra long-haul routes. The fuselage was stretched by 14ft 1in (4.3m), and the fuel capacity was 50 per cent more than the -300 series. The tail fin and horizontal stabilizer were increased in size. To support the extra weight, the centre line undercarriage was changed to a four-wheel bogie. Power came from four Rolls-Royce Trent 553 turbofans with an output of 54,00lb st each. Pictured at Dubai International Airport, in November 2008, is Airbus A340-541 A6-ERG c/n 608 of locally based Emirates, the first operator of the variant. In March 2009, this aircraft was damaged by a tail strike on take-off at Melbourne. The incorrect gross weight had been set by the flight crew. It was repaired, and in 2014 it was withdrawn from use in Lourdes and later broken up.

Airliners of the 2000s

The A340-600 series first flew in April 2001, and operations started with Virgin Atlantic in August of the following year. It was 39ft 4in (12m) longer than the -300 series. The engines were Rolls-Royce Trent 556 turbofans with an output of 56,000lb st each. Pictured climbing away from Cape Town International Airport, in September 2006, is Airbus A340-642 ZS-SNB c/n 417 of Johannesburg-based SAA (South African Airways). This aircraft was put into store at the company base in 2018.

Arriving at Johannesburg O. R. Tambo International Airport, in September 2006, is Airbus A340-642 EC-JCY c/n 617 of Madrid-based Spanish flag carrier Iberia. This aircraft was withdrawn from use in 2019 and then broken up in Teruel, Spain.

Airliners of the 2000s

The A380 is the world's largest passenger airliner. It first flew in April 2005 and has a full-length double-deck. In the usual three-class seating, it will carry over 500 passengers and has a maximum certified load of 853 people. Its range is 8,000 miles (14,800km). Production has now ceased, and the last one built was delivered to the largest user, Emirates, in December 2021. Pictured in July 2009, at Oshkosh Wittman Regional Airport, Wisconsin, is Airbus A380-841 F-WWDD c/n 004, operated by the Airbus Test Fleet. This aircraft has been preserved at the Musee de l'Air Paris since 2017.

It was a sad day for many when, in October 2003, British Airways took Concorde out of service. It flew higher and faster than any other airliner has ever done or is likely to ever do in the near future. Pictured at London Heathrow, in July 2002, is BAe/Aérospatiale Concorde 102 G-BOAE c/n 212 of British Airways. This aircraft has been preserved at Grantley Adams International Airport, Barbados.

Other books you might like:

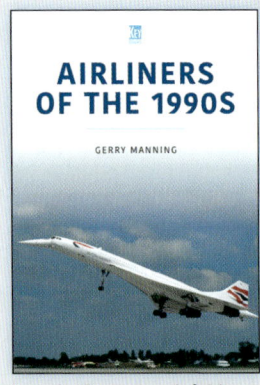
Historic Commercial Aircraft Series, Vol. 4

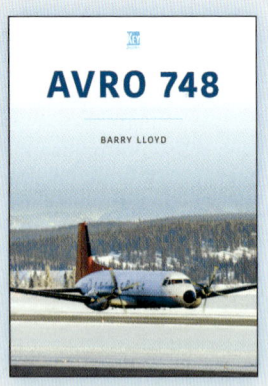
Historic Commercial Aircraft Series, Vol. 3

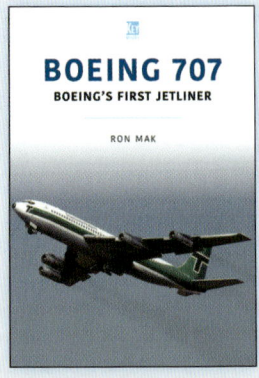
Historic Commercial Aircraft Series, Vol. 2

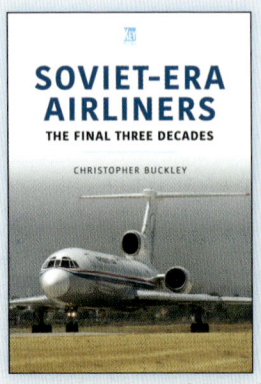
Historic Commercial Aircraft Series, Vol. 1

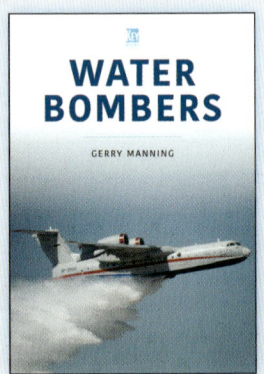

For our full range of titles please visit:
shop.keypublishing.com/books

VIP Book Club

Sign up today and receive
TWO FREE E-BOOKS

Be the first to find out about our forthcoming book releases and receive exclusive offers.

Register now at **keypublishing.com/vip-book-club**

Our VIP Book Club is a 100% spam-free zone, and we will never share your email with anyone else. You can read our full privacy policy at: privacy.keypublishing.com